"*Leading and Managing Simultan*... aspiring leaders and managers to ...... business. With candid personal and professional advice, Mark Hubble highlights the attributes and actions you need to build high-performing teams and improve customer experience while improving loyalty of those you serve and those who serve with you."

—RON KAUFMAN,
New York Times Bestselling Author, *Uplifting Service*

"Mark covers a large range of business and management topics and I can envision this becoming a must read for aspiring managers and leaders."

—ALFRED VIEHBECK, PhD,
DOW 30 Company Research Director (retired)

"Mark's proven approach to strategic focus, new business development, and creating new products and services are quite impressive and yield tangible results. Its works! He successfully developed and coached his numerous teams and now articulates his methodology to readers as a how to guide to ultimate success. This is a must read as to the importance of value creation and ultimate business sustainability."

—STEVE CASLEY,
Global Business Executive, Travel and Hospitality, PREMISE

"This book is a very respectful, insightful guide to get the best out of you. I stop at each Lessons Learned and I love them all. I also like the end of chapter questions as they give me time to reflect on myself. This is the underlying magic of this book and what makes it different. Mark has turned his experiences into over 125 Lessons Learned and many other insightful tips. Try it and you will see… as his work is absolutely amazing, and quite energizing! Thank you Mark for putting this book together."

—STEPHANIE SIOUFFI-VAREILHES,
Director, IATA Training

"I've read this book and am impressed. Thanks for the privilege of reading it. I can see the benefits of your having read so widely throughout your career. It comes through in every chapter loud and clear! In your Lessons Learned boxes, the most compelling ones are when you are telling vivid stories about your own experiences. Such gems set your book apart from the many other Leadership and Management books out there."

—ALEKSANDER POPOVICH,
Strategic Advisor, Catch the Solution

"What wonderful wisdom you share. You successfully deliver the key ingredients, recipe and building blocks in a how-to guide that any aspiring leader should want to understand, and more experienced leaders will benefit from gaining another perspective. Mark's introspective Lessons Learned and end of chapter questions are also an effective learning tool."

—JACK CALHOUN,
Publisher and Editorial Director

"A must read! It offers a thorough business foundation and comprehensive career guide. I gained many great insights and learned much along the way. Its presentation is thoughtful and has a logical structure as to how each chapter builds upon itself. I appreciate how Mark has his readers challenges themselves after each chapter. Questions are presented to get the reader to self-reflect as to their own personal and business understanding. My favorite part is the Lessons Learned, where Mark brings in his own personal experiences as real-life examples, and not just theory."

—STERLING P. HORNBUCKLE,
Director of Business Development

"Congratulations Mark. I have read many books related to change management, cultural behaviors, etc., but yours is different as it is more practical and useful. You have put a lot of wisdom, knowledge, and passion into your book. I enjoyed reading it and learned a lot through your numerous anecdotes and Lessons Learned. This book definitely adds value to its reader as it combines theoretical knowledge with your own personal experiences. It will assist aspiring professionals in understanding leadership, management and business acumen in practical terms."

—GÜNTHER MATSCHNIGG,
SVP Safety, Operations and Infrastructure, IATA (retired)

"This book is a perfect reference and summary as to what you need to know about commercial leadership and success. I really like your coverage of Ansoff and growth strategies. Most business challenges can be solved by looking at the 4 P's and the Ansoff Matrix. I also like the short and concise chapters, with the brief summaries and Lessons Learned, and the though-provoking questions."

—TIM-JASPER SCHAAF,
Director Marketing and Sales, IATA

"Awesome! I look forward to reading and learning more. This is a smooth read, and it makes me want to continue learning."

—JOHN D. HICKS,
Premier Banker AVP, Wells Fargo Bank

"I like this a lot! The format, particularly where Mark ends each chapter with questions that challenges the reader to use your book as input in their perianal life/work worlds. I also think this format can be turned into a proper e-learning/class course."

—HASSAN AURAG,
Board of Advisors, TrekSecure

"I wish I had this how to guide when I was in the military as something I could have shared with my subordinates."

—ROBERT HOYLE,
United States Air Force, Senior Non-Commissioned Officer (retired)

Leading and Managing
Simultaneously

Leading and Managing
Simultaneously
Lessons Learned in Global Business

Mark R. Hubble

Charleston, SC
www.PalmettoPublishing.com

*Leading and Managing Simultaneously:
Lessons Learned in Global Business*

Copyright © 2022 by Mark R. Hubble

All rights reserved

No portion of this book may be reproduced, stored in a retrieval system, or transmitted in any form by any means–electronic, mechanical, photocopy, recording, or other–except for brief quotations in printed reviews, without prior permission of the author.

First Edition

Hardcover ISBN: 979-8-88590-446-9
Paperback ISBN: 979-8-88590-447-6
eBook ISBN: 979-8-88590-448-3

Table of Contents

Preface xiii
Part 1: Leadership 1
Chapter 1: Effective Leadership Defined 3
    Leadership Principles 8
    Core Values 10
Chapter 2: Leadership Styles 15
    Democratic 16
    Autocratic 17
    Laissez-Faire 17
    Transformational 18
    Visionary 19
    Coaching 19
    Affiliative 20
    Pacesetting 20
    Commanding 21
Chapter 3: Leadership Attributes 25
    Communication 26
    Humor 29
    Humility 29
    Character 30
    Emotional Quotient (EI) vs. Intelligence Quotient (IQ) 31
    Cultural Intelligence 34
    Charisma 36
    Integrity 37
    Conscientiousness 38
Chapter 4: Leadership Work Environment 43
    Vision 45
    Mission 46

Coaching and Mentoring	50
Succession Planning	53
Cultural Diversity and Inclusion	55
Skill Set Diversity	59
Social Responsibility	60
Chapter 5: Leadership and Strategy	**63**
Strategic Intent	63
Organizational Design	71
Organizational Structure Types	72
Chapter 6: Leadership and the Customer	**79**
The Customer Experience	80
Customer Service	81
Customer Satisfaction	85
Customer Loyalty	88
Chapter 7: Leadership and Innovation: Process and Product	**93**
Part 2: Management	**105**
Chapter 8: Effective Management Defined	**107**
Management Principles	107
Planning	114
Organizing	115
Directing	116
Control	117
Chapter 9: Management Styles	**119**
Autocratic	120
Authoritative	120
Persuasive	120
Paternalistic	121
Democratic	121
Consultative	121
Participative	122
Collaborative	122

Table of Contents

    Visionary 122
    Transformational 122
    Coaching 123
    Laissez-Faire 124
    Delegative 124
    Transactional 124
    Pacesetting. 125
Chapter 10: Management Attributes 127
    Communication 127
    Networking 131
    Stakeholder Management 132
    Performance Management. 134
    Time Management. 138
    Negotiating 140
Chapter 11: Management Work Environment. 145
    Business Fundamentals 146
    Work Environment 149
    Building High-Performance Teams 150
    Strategic Focus. 154
Chapter 12: Management Decision-Making 161
    Strategic Decision-Making 163
    Operational Decision-Making 164
Chapter 13: Business Growth Drivers 171
    Market Penetration 172
    Market Development. 172
    New Product Development 173
    Diversification 177
    Partnerships. 178
    Mergers and Acquisitions 180
    Value Creation. 182
    Quality. 183

Chapter 14: Financial Management 187
    Income Statement 190
    Balance Sheet 194
    Cashflow Statement 196
    Additional Financial Activities 197
Chapter 15: Managing the Four Ps 203
    Product 203
    Price 208
    Promotion 211
    Place 213
Chapter 16: Sales and Marketing 217
    Sales Management 218
    Sales Acumen 219
    Sales Operations 223
    Marketing Management 225
    Product Marketing 228
    Marketing Research 228
    Social Media 229
    Advertising 229
    Digital Marketing 230
    Corporate Marketing 230
    Public Relations (PR) 231
    Branding 231
    Future Trends 235
Part 3: Post-Script 239
    Planning Your Future 241
    Author Bio 245
    Bibliography 247

Preface

This book is written for those who aspire to grow personally and develop professionally, those who understand that true success can only be achieved if you act diligently to better yourself and others around you. Many people fail to meet their full potential in life because they stop learning or listening to others.

In your personal life, the road to success begins by focusing on yourself first and making the necessary changes from within. How can you become a better person? This involves your mind in deciding what you will do and your heart in deciding why you should do it. In your business life, success can be achieved by building, managing, and leading high-performance teams with the goal of maximizing their efforts and outcomes.

My intent is to provide you with numerous insights, ideas, suggestions, guidance, and techniques that have assisted me during my lifelong journey. I will share with you the necessary skill sets, personal attributes, and various styles that are at your disposal within the context of leadership and management. The ultimate choice is yours, so choose your path wisely.

My goal will be achieved by improving your overall knowledge and understanding of two important disciplines: leadership and management. Leadership is focused on creating an aspirational and compelling future articulated in your vision statement addressing why we are here and where we want to go. Management encompasses all current operational aspects of your daily business. It addresses what you will deliver and how related it is to your mission statement. Applying what you learn and choose to take away should increase your chances of future success; it has for me.

Let me briefly explain my broad and multifaceted professional background, as this is the foundation for the learning concepts I will reference throughout this book. Upon my graduation from the business school of Texas State University in 1983, I began my career in sales in the regions of central and south Texas. We assisted professors and their students with textbook and software support focused on business curriculums. In 1986, while still working in sales, I earned my MBA at St. Edward's University in Austin, Texas. Twelve years later and having held numerous additional managerial positions in both sales and product sides of the business, I became the youngest president and CEO of that same organization. Since then, and over the past thirty-seven years, I have had the challenge and pleasure to hold additional "C-Suite" (CEO, president, Sr. VP) leadership roles across five distinct industry segments: educational publishing, software, financial services, academia, and aviation.

My global experience, cultural awakening, and overall understanding have been shaped by spending quality time with many great and intriguing people from every part of the world. My business acumen has been acquired by leading and managing many key business functions, including sales, marketing, customer service, product management/development, finance, procurement, information technology, e-commerce, legal, human resources and strategy.

My "hands-on" line-of-business experience extends across the following product and service categories: business data analytics and intelligence, training, accreditation and certification, consulting, publishing, electronic settlement systems, conferences and events, strategic partnerships, as well as travel and tourism.

The annual revenues of my former organizations ranged from thirty million dollars to in excess of three hundred million dollars. But more important than the size of an organization are the unique external challenges it faces and the internal complexities that need to be successfully navigated and overcome.

The operating profit margins of the organizations I led were among the industry's highest with one averaging in excess of 60 percent for over ten years.

These industry-leading financial results were fueled by my team's applied creativity, passion to innovate, willingness to take calculated risks, diligent work ethic, and unrelenting commitment to shared successes. Their efforts led to the creation of numerous compelling, market-leading new products and services, strategic partnerships, as well as the continuous implementation of many internal efficiency and productivity processes.

Putting financial successes aside, the most rewarding part of my career has been the time and effort I have spent guiding, developing, teaching, coaching, and mentoring others. Over time, I have become a good judge of my colleague's character and their willingness to learn and change, or not. As there is only so much time in a day, I suggest you spend it wisely with the right colleagues.

Being an educator at heart, I am a huge supporter of continuous learning to regularly challenge my own beliefs and those of others, at any cost. Former president of Harvard University, Derek Bok, once stated: "If you think education is expensive, try ignorance." [1] While this statement may come across as strong or harsh to some, it does beg the question as to the opportunity costs potentially associated with not furthering your education. When considering your education, I suggest you always choose to "opt in" and pay the price as it's well worth it in the long run.

I am always eager to learn and share new concepts and theories. More importantly, I enjoy the pragmatic testing of these in live, real-world settings to validate their applicability. While many of these theories look good on paper, when applied in a business scenario, they do not always work as planned. As the saying goes, in life, there are no "dress rehearsals" and rarely do you get a second chance. On the other hand, if you never take risks, you will never learn new things.

Another goal of this book is to highlight proven leadership and management principles and practices that led to the very successful financial and operating results of my prior teams and organizations. These concepts are applicable at many organizational levels to reach a broader reading audience. Whether you are a younger professional with less experience who is aspiring to move into a management or leadership role, or you are currently in such a role and want to gain new insights to prepare for your next move up the corporate ladder, there are numerous recommendations for both.

My approach in this book is to first establish a solid foundation in business and commercial functions. As we will address the most important business functions, I am confident you will find many of them interesting and compelling. Each topic is presented in a similar format (concepts, definitions, theories, importance, examples, etc.) to ensure you reach a minimum level of business acumen, knowledge, and comprehension before putting them into practice within the disciplines of leadership and management. As we will cover much material, to assist you along this educational path, I begin each chapter with a "Preview" of what's ahead to set your learning expectations.

This book is brimming with numerous critical success factors relating to the most relevant leadership and management principles and practices. For greater reinforcement, I also share my own personal stories, views, analogies, and advice in the form of "Lessons Learned" along my exciting and rewarding journey. (Both good and bad experiences!) In addition, and in support of other important topics, I weave in hundreds of more actual, pragmatic, real-world examples. All these examples, experiences, and stories are deidentified for the privacy, protection, and fairness to others.

Each chapter ends with an interactive section titled "What are your thoughts…" I pose numerous questions capturing the essence of key business, leadership, and management concepts and principles.

You (the reader), and at your discretion, can then elaborate on how to apply these and why, given various personal and business situations in your own life.

Many business scholars do not always agree that the skill sets and attributes that make a successful leader are similar to those of a successful manager. But in fact, they may differ. Here in lies the leadership-management paradox. Still, while one of these disciplines cannot replace the other, I firmly believe you can excel at both! However, just because you are, or have been, a top individual performer does not necessarily guarantee you similar success when it comes to managing and leading others. I totally support this premise and have witnessed firsthand top individual performers fail when promoted to the next level.

For example, a star athlete is not always "fit" to lead, manage, or coach their team. The same can be said for top sales performers as well as many other functional roles. The key is to successfully transition yourself from being individually driven to team driven, which is no small task. Being self-motivated is one thing, but can you successfully shift your own mindset to inspire, motivate, develop, coach, and mentor others? Your past individual successes become irrelevant, as it is now about team success.

Is such a personal and business transformation possible? I say "YES," as these concepts can be learned. If I can do it, so can you.

Going back to the star athlete example, they spend a lot of time practicing and less time performing. Yet, business professionals and executives usually spend little to no time practicing and all their time performing. In general, most business professionals and executives short themselves in learning how to lead more effectively.

Before becoming a leader, you can increase your chances of success by growing yourself first. Once a leader, it becomes about growing others. I strongly believe that individuals can simultaneously succeed at both leading and managing others. An experienced leader possesses the abilities to inspire and guide a team's direction as well as masterfully plan, organize, assist, and support the same team with its execution. Such a combined undertaking takes a lot of time, effort, commitment, and trial and error on your part. Therefore, possessing and combining strong leadership abilities, "plus" having strong management skills, "equals" success—a winning "equation."

I want to thank a few of those who trusted and believed in me by offering exciting and challenging personal and business opportunities throughout my career, including Timothy McEwen, Larry Jones, Martin Kenny, Ronald Schaffer, John Leddo and Giovanni Bisignani.

I also want to recognize the many academic scholars and business experts whose lifelong research and important publications have informed my business acumen and helped shape me into who I am today. I reference their breakthrough contributions and/or insightful quotes throughout this book. These individuals include, but are not limited to, Warren Benis and Robert Townsend, Robert Kaplan, John Maxwell (leadership), Debra Ancona (leadership, organizational theory, and team processes), Robert Weiler (leadership development and organizational design), Michael Porter, Jack Welch, C.K. Prahalad, and Gary Hamil (strategy), Pankaj Ghemawat (global strategy), Peter Drucker and Colin Powell (management), Philip Kotler (marketing), Bill Morrison (international sales strategies), Ron Kaufman (customer experience/service), Clayton Christensen (innovation), Krishna Palepu and Paul Healy (business financial statement analysis), Carl Warren (financial accounting), Daniel Goleman, Richard Boyatis, Annie McKee (emotional intelligence), David Livermore (cultural intelligence), Kevin Keller (branding), David Brooks, Stephen Covey, and John Wooden (character, wisdom and improving oneself), Kevin Dobby (qualitative coaching), and Chilina Hills (communications and international speaking coach).

Over my career, I have been blessed to be surrounded by many unique and diverse high-performance team members whose shared passion, efforts, and total commitment to our inspiring mandate led us to great business successes and much personal fulfilment. I consider many to be great friends and part of my extended family, and I thank them all for the numerous contributions they have made to this book.

Thank you also to my editor, Russel Buche, for his valuable feedback and encyclopedic knowledge of business concepts and the English language, a rare combination. His patience and coaching were greatly appreciated.

Lastly, I want to recognize and thank my number one fan and supporter, as well as my strongest critic, my spouse Debi. Throughout my career, she has been my "rock," sounding board, best friend, and soul mate. She always pushed me to new heights. This book is personally dedicated to Debi. Over the past thirty-five years of marriage, we made many personal sacrifices due to my long work hours and hectic travel schedule. Debi held down the fort at home, taking care of everything, which allowed me to focus on my job. Looking back, I know Debi would agree we have no regrets, and given the opportunity to relive our past, we would live it exactly the same way and not change a thing.

> **Lessons Learned**
>
> If you believe you have nothing new to learn, or have no interest in doing so, please move on or retire. Unfortunately, you are in the way of others and holding them back from fulfilling their own dreams. Or, maybe, this book might inspire you!

Part 1

Leadership

CHAPTER 1

Effective Leadership Defined

Chapter Preview

- How to lead with your mind and heart
- Which personal traits and qualities successful leaders share
- Distinguishing characteristics of a strong leader vs. an average leader.
- How to ascend to the pinnacle of leadership greatness
- Practical advice to begin or continue your leadership journey.
- Why your personal and professional values and behaviors should align

> **Lessons Learned**
> The first person you lead is yourself and then others.

Leadership is about creating a longer term and aspirational future state and guiding your team toward this. Being a role model, here, is key for a leader, then establishing an efficient decision-making process to prioritize which focal points come first to achieve it. Leadership is considered by many to be an art based on philosophy rather than a quantitative science. It is more qualitative in nature and less about the numbers. Thus, it is a discipline that is less "black and white" with little uniformity yet is gray and intuitive.

Becoming a quality leader is quite difficult to master, as there is no single rule book to play by or only one right way to lead. However, there are numerous common attributes, traits, skill sets, and styles that most successful leaders share and apply. It is up to each individual leader to shape and define their own role based on who they are, what they stand for and how they consistently act and behave relative to their own unique personality, background, and experience.

Leaders inspire forward movement and drive change through innovation. As Mahatma Gandhi once said, "Be the change you wish to see." His message was very clear, change can only come from within each of us.

Typically, leaders with high IQs (intelligence quotient) lead with their heads while leaders with high EI (emotional intelligence) lead with their hearts. The strongest and most successful leaders utilize both. They establish trust through their competence, their ability to connect with others through strong interpersonal relationships, and they possess observable personal integrity.

Leaders live by a code of conduct based on a clear set of ethics, morals, ideals, and values. As Robert Kaplan stated, "Figure out what you believe is the truth, act on these beliefs and bring value to others." [2] Ethical boundaries are the lines that true leaders will never cross for personal financial gain. Unfair business practices, illegal transactions, or manipulative economic dilemmas are anathema to true leaders. And these beliefs are quite apparent to all their followers.

Quality leaders possess a high level of integrity, empathy, loyalty, and decisiveness. They empower others, take action, and never waiver. Leaders understand it is more about what they do vs. what they say. Leaders think with an entrepreneurial mindset, acting as an "owner" and pushing others to think beyond their own set of responsibilities. Everyone should put the needs of their organization first.

Leaders are direct, honest, transparent, "tell it like it is," yet exude fairness, kindness, and compassion. Leaders are also inquisitive. Per Simon Sinek, effective leaders start with "why" we are here, "what" we hope to accomplish, and "how" we shall succeed. [3] The "why" is what guides us to personal and professional fulfillment and drives our behaviors. It's less about what you do, but more about why you do it.

Leadership is not based on a position or title, rather it is the leader who makes the position. They shape their own role. It is not about one's own power, but the ability to empower others. Their authority to lead is earned, not given. This requires mutual trust and respect between a leader and their team. Typically, your own career advancement will be limited if you cannot work with and through others. Because, as you grow and take on additional responsibilities in the scope of your work, you can no longer continue to do everything yourself. A team effort will be required.

> **Lessons Learned**
>
> Empowering others does not free the empoweree of the ultimate accountability. When empowering others, we still own the ultimate outcome. We cannot relinquish it or point blame elsewhere if things do not go as planned.

Another common leadership trait is self-confidence. A leader treats everyone as their equal. On the contrary, if a leader possesses certain insecurities, these will hamper their empowerment abilities as they may fear that successfully coaching and mentoring others' growth and development might lead to their displacement. This is a very short-sighted, restrictive, and naïve way to think.

Leaders alone accomplish nothing. It is their followers' strengths that matter, which must be consistently and regularly recognized with praise. As two Navy Seal leaders, Jocko Willink and Leif Badin stated, "There are not bad teams, just bad leaders." [4] Strong leaders utilize their abilities to effectively influence and persuade others while bringing out their team's hidden potential. Per Napoleon Bonaparte, "Leaders are dealers in hope."

Are all successful leaders created equally? Or are there varying levels that leaders can ascend to, becoming more and more successful as they develop their own inner abilities? To the first question, I say "no." To address the second question, John Maxwell thoughtfully and accurately developed a five-tier sequence of levels to which a leader can ascend. [5] As leaders develop and grow personally and professionally, they have a greater impact on their people and organization at each of the higher levels. This is driven by the leader's continued growth in their personal competencies and overall leadership abilities. Keep in mind, these levels are not clear cut, distinct, or even known to the leader themselves or everyone else but are more subtle as everyone moves upwards. The levels are more about the positive impacts and broader reach that the leader is achieving. The levels (from bottom to top, or basic to advanced) are:

- Level 1—Leadership anointed by "Position" does not make the leader. While your authority may be recognized, others will follow you because they think they must, not because they want to. As a leader, the key question to ask yourself at this level is "do you possess the ability to influence others beyond your job description?" If this is true, you will ascend to Level 2.

- Level 2—"Permission" occurs when you begin to focus on people and their "on-the-job" skill sets needed for success. The same goes for yourself! Your team's trust in you deepens based on your influence and your colleagues' belief in you. They now want to follow you. Energy levels pick up and the work environment becomes more enjoyable. Channels of communication are open and honest with a balance of candor and care. As the old saying goes,

"People go along with leaders they get along with." At this level, as a leader, you begin to make room at the top by putting your high-potential, future leaders in new situations. Hopefully you are now ready for Level 3.

- Level 3—At this "Production" level, additional focus is put on improving individual and organizational skills, productivity, and results. This level is all about making things happen. Momentum is created and, if successful, your team's credibility and confidence in you continues to grow. This sets the foundation for team building to occur. You are now ready to ascend to Level 4.

- Level 4—"People Development" encompasses the formal establishment of new leaders within your ranks. This occurs due to the time, effort, energy, and capital you have invested in their long-term future. It is now about organizational sustainability by developing new, future leaders. Allowing them to lead on their own, ensuring they are put into the right positions while empowering them should all occur at this point. You can now transition and become a good follower and "lead by being led" by others you have groomed.

- Level 5—This is the "Pinnacle" of leadership that only a few (a fortunate handful) ever reach. These are the "one percenters." At this level, your work has benefited everyone you have touched over your career. You have earned and are bestowed the ultimate respect and gratitude of your peers. It is now about the legacy you will leave and how you will be remembered.

If you aspire to reach this leadership pinnacle, how do you go about it and where do you start? Robert Kaplan quite succinctly lays out a high-level, logical, pragmatic, and practical process to start your journey. [2] These steps include:

- Set a clear vision and priorities. Agree upon what drives your organization every day. Focus on this and this only.

- Prioritize all tasks needing to be executed at the highest quality levels that make your organization unique.

- Regularly communicate your vision and priorities to your staff.

- Align all actions, efforts, and decisions to support, assist, and deliver your vision and priorities. Monitor progress and adjust as needed.

- Implement an organization structure that details what positions are needed with what skill sets and which individuals "fit" into these critical positions. Agree upon the ideal and critical leadership and management styles, aptitudes, behaviors, and values these individuals must possess. The leader must be a role model.

- Make timely and decisive decisions, remembering passion drives performance.

In summary, influencing requires great communication, which leads to recognition. Recognition leads to the ability to influence loyal followers. By developing and empowering others, a leader's lasting value is succession. When a strong leader eventually departs, they will have left their organization in a better condition than when they found it in.

The following are other key leadership focal points and principles which I believe strongly in and have successfully utilized.

Leadership Principles

Leaders should set a consistent, aspirational tone, corporate culture, and shared values. Everyone within your organization should understand and embrace the greater good as to why we are here and what we want to achieve. Ask yourself, "What actions and behaviors emulate your own values?" More important, "What role does each individual play in making our corporate vision become reality?" If everyone cannot see it, they cannot seize it.

An inspiring vision will define how the future will look. It should be far reaching, going beyond any one individual. Such a vision will attract others like a magnet to follow it and bring their own resources to bear. The vision requires a strategic focus and should not be too general as to its interpretation.

Successful leaders possess the following personal beliefs and traits in common:

> **Lessons Learned**
>
> I also aspire and try to live diligently by these principles. Building character is a lifelong journey. Do we truly understand and accept our purpose in life? This question gets to the heart of one's character. It is more about our big picture contributions and less about our individual accomplishments. Trust me, I still find myself being sucked into the latter.

- Doing the right things and putting people first (a qualitative people focus).

- Utilizing practical and well-grounded considerations (e.g., realistic, sensible) vs. being solely conceptual or theoretical.

- Honesty: Freely admitting "I know what I do not know."

- Character: Having integrity makes trust possible and trust makes leadership possible. Everyone's moral compass is unique from all others. Colleagues want to know who their leaders are and what they stand for. This draws from past experiences, both successes and failures. Our character is built around a combination of many personal qualities, both good and bad.

Remember, "A goal is a dream with a deadline." What are your goals? If your personal goals overreach your corporate goals, your chances of ultimate success are heightened. I have always stretched my personal goals much higher than my corporate targets. For example, as a salesperson, if I received a three-million-dollar sales target, my personal target would be six million dollars. As a CEO, if we planned to grow revenues by 6 percent, I set an aspirational goal at 8 percent. The ultimate purpose was to not disappoint others. As I look back, this view was not always the healthiest way of thinking. Colleagues under too much pressure or stress to perform tend to not do so well. Finding a work-and-life balance works best.

Core Values

Our personal and professional values must align, otherwise we run the risk of sending conflicting messages to others. Jack Welch [6] articulated what he looked for in leaders by way of a simple formula expressed as, "4E + 1P":

Lessons Learned

Better understand yourself before trying to understand others. Change yourself first. One way to do this is to become an enabler by changing or stop doing something that you have always done. This can be a common leadership, management, or business habit that needs improvement. Or you can start something new, outside your comfort zone. The key is to pick something that no one would expect from you. Allow your team to witness this change in public. This shows everyone that you are not above the change you are asking from them. If you can do it, so can they.

For example, I committed to try to no longer jump in quickly and provide my solutions to my colleagues' questions. I realized I was doing their mental work and problem-solving for them. Little learning was taking place with this approach. I promised to be more patient by coaching them and asking them thoughtful questions until they came up with their own conclusions. I began to witness firsthand that once a colleague believed they were a bigger part of the solution, their commitment to passionately deliver grew immensely. However, I must add that this new behavior was difficult for me to do at first, as I had always enjoyed sharing what I "thought" I knew. However, I soon realized if I had continued my former behavior, we would all think alike, which would have been quite boring.

- **Energy**—Thrive on action. Be relentless.

- **Energize others**—This can be contagious.

- **Edge**—Show the courage to make tough decisions and take calculated risks.

- **Execute**—The ability to successfully get the job done.

- **Passion**—People with passion care, are authentic, and excited about their work.

I support this formula and find it easy to embrace. The principles and core values that guide my professional and personal life can be summed up in the following three:

> **Lessons Learned**
>
> If you are not risking your job, you are not doing your job. As a wise person once said, "Your comfort zone is great place, but nothing grows there." Push the envelope! On the other hand, poor leaders possess some common characteristics. They can be abrasive, arrogant, untrustworthy, self-centered, risk averse, deliver poor results, and are lacking in delegation, empowerment abilities, as well as people skills. Have you witnessed these behaviors before? Such leaders are difficult to follow. But the good news is their past eventually catches up to them and they move on.

Trust—It is the foundation of personal relationships and makes leading possible. Without trust, there is no permanent foundation for long-term success. Leaders must not simply talk about trust; they must build it. You cannot talk your way out of every situation; you should behave and act your way out. Trust is one of the highest forms of motivation for others. Empower others as you will not always be together (i.e., in the same location). Practice loyalty and have each other's back. Trust is earned, not imposed.

Respect—Treat everyone with respect. Respect should be mutual. If not, the end of personal relationships, if not the business itself, is inevitable. People tend to not stay around others they do not respect. Just as with trust, respect is also earned, not just forced. I find it quite challenging to spend time with those I do not respect. No respect, no relationship.

Early in my career, a colleague gave me some simple yet solid advice that still resonates with me today. He said, "Unless you cannot avoid it, do not work with jerks!" (I have toned down his quote somewhat as to not offend anyone). His main point was that life is too short to spend time with people you do not respect.

> **Lessons Learned**
>
> Reward and celebrate the right behaviors and actions within your team. There are many ways to do this that are not expensive but are totally appreciated. This can be as simple as recognizing those who live your corporate values (e.g., by acting as a role model) during company meetings. Giving out small gift coupons or certificates and announcing awards via your intranet site for all colleagues to view. Personal, hand-written "thank you" notes, and acknowledgements also go a long way toward showing colleagues you care. On the contrary, calling out misbehaving colleagues in public may only fuel their anger and encourage them to act up more (similar to an unruly child).

Therefore, try to spend it with those whose company you enjoy, respect, care about, or love.

> **Lessons Learned**
>
> Try not to micromanage others, but know the details of their work. If you find yourself micromanaging, ask yourself why. Is it a lack of understanding of the task at hand? Or a staff skill gap issue on their part? Or a lack of trust on your part? Or are you being controlling, not allowing them to do their job? And the reverse can also be true. If you are being micromanaged, it begs the questions, "If my boss is doing my job for me, why? Is this a trust issue or am I truly not needed?" I suggest you find answers to these questions promptly.

What are your thoughts?
Do you lead with IQ, EI, or both (and provide examples)?

Write your personal code of ethics. What core values drive your behaviors?

Commitment—If you give, you shall receive. But receiving is not always instant gratification. Commitment is situational and varies from day to day. There are peaks and valleys. At times, you give 100 percent and get zero back (and vice versa) due to what is currently occurring within and around you and your colleagues, friends, or your partners. It is rarely a 50/50 sharing all the time. Think long term; be patient, understanding, and forgiving when things are not always going as you expect or prefer. Commitment directly aligns with empowerment; usually, staff that are more empowered are more committed.

> **Lessons Learned**
>
> In my view, such personal values and attributes should be exhibited consistently, whether you are at work or at home. These are not to be turned on or off based on your setting.

When undertaking an initiative, do you start by first addressing the "what and why" or "why and how?" Explain your methodology.

Related to Maxwell's 5-tier sequences of leadership growth, where are you now and what are your plans to ascend to the next level?

In a few sentences, can you articulate your purpose in life?

What are your personal and professional goals over the next one, three, and five years?

CHAPTER 2

Leadership Styles

Chapter Preview

- **When and why the nine leadership styles should be practiced and their pros and cons.**
- **Choose the style(s) that best fits within your comfort zone and personality.**
- **The importance of "authenticity" as a leader.**
- **Which set of "soft skills" can enable your success**

A leadership style is a personal method of providing direction and guidance, implementing plans, and motivating staff. Many styles exist across the leadership spectrum. Your and your team's future success depends on your style choices. As General "Stonewall" Jackson stated, "You may be whatever you resolve to be." Thus, I say, choose wisely.

A good starting point is to ask your team the following questions about you:

- What is (are) your most useful and favorable leadership style(s) and which is (are) not? Examples should be welcomed.

- What specific styles do not exist within you that should be considered and why?

- Whether you agree with your team's input or not is not important, as their perceptions are reality.

Whatever set of styles you embrace and adopt, being an "authentic" leader is critical for them to be well received. Being empathetic, genuine, transparent, and honest will assist you in building the key leadership ingredient of trust. Being viewed by others as "authentic" involves your ability to be self-aware, knowing your strengths and weaknesses while continuously reassessing them. Admit your mistakes and take responsibility for them. Being well balanced when processing all views under your consideration, while being open and honest when sharing your opinions, is also important. Having the ability to offer constructive comments without offending others is another trait to authenticity. The needs of your organization and its people come first. Sorry, but your own needs as the leader come in a distant third in my view.

As I said, there are numerous styles to choose from. They each have their purpose and reason for being, based on the leader's own unique personality and comfort zone. The chosen style should also relate to the specific business situation occurring. Let's review the most common styles in use today, why they usually come into action, as well as a few pros and cons of each.

Democratic

Also known as "participative," the democratic leadership style values staff input and gaining commitment through their participation. This style is deployed when the leader may be uncertain as to what future direction to undertake. Or they know the direction themselves but want to lead and guide their staff collaboratively toward it. To accomplish this approach, the leader plays a facilitator role and must be a good listener.

This style is widely accepted, is successful, and can be quite motivational for staff, increasing their satisfaction levels and creativity. But beware of a few of its drawbacks. Building consensus can be very time-consuming, which could be detrimental if your situation dictates moving with speed. Also, a few strong and aggressive staff personalities can dominate the majority. Thus, in practice, the majority may not always rule. I have witnessed and utilized this style, and I am supportive of it and good results were achieved. I suggest you avoid this style during times of crisis.

Autocratic

This "authoritative" style is preferred by leaders making decisions on their own with limited to no input coming from others. It is an extreme version of the "transactional" management style (see Chapter 9), which focuses on paying for and rewarding the performance as well as punishing poor performers. The autocratic leader rules with an iron fist and their communications take the form of a one-way monologue, not an interactive two-way dialogue. Control on the part of the leader is very apparent and they exhibit little flexibility. There may also be a big "fear factor" among the staff. Examples of autocratic leaders include Vladimir Putin and Napoleon Bonaparte.

Most of your colleagues who feel they have a vested interest in the future will not welcome or appreciate this style, particularly when not in a crisis mode. Morale goes down, staff resentment goes up, and high turnover and absenteeism is apparent. However, strong performance and output can result, but may be short-lived. I have witnessed this style with mixed results and have rarely used it.

Laissez-Faire

This style is named from the French and means "let them do" or "let it go." This style should bring true empowerment to your team as the leader does not micromanage them. This sounds good in principle, but not always in practice. Some form of framework should guide the leader and the team. Otherwise, ambiguity can result as management's role definitions may not be clear. This can freeze the actions of their respective staff.

An experienced team of professionals may like this style and proactively run with it. However, most others may perceive and believe the leader is just sitting on the sidelines, as the leader's participation is low to nonexistent. For such a style to work, the leader needs to set clear goals, actively monitor team performance, and clearly communicate their expectations regularly.

Empowerment does not relieve the leader of accountability for the ultimate outcome. Therefore, some leaders will step in if they strongly disagree with the proposed solutions being offered and send their team back to the drawing board to start over. This can not only waste a lot of staff time but drive up their frustration levels. Such an approach can easily backfire, and I have witnessed this style being executed with poor results. However, Warren Buffet proves this style can be successful as well.

Transformational

This approach may be useful for those leaders needing to drive change and continuous process improvement or create an environment of innovation. Jeff Bezos is a successful leader who fits this profile. Being a charismatic leader, who communicates effectively and can inspire staff, will only help your cause.

Driving change may require that some prior corporate policies and procedures be revised, strengthened, or relaxed to accommodate a new way of thinking, behaving, and operating. As you may be trying to shift the whole corporate culture, do not underestimate the enormity of this task. The alternative of doing nothing, however, is not the answer.

When it comes to driving transformation, I always start from the exact same point: building the "case for change." This case must be discussed, understood, and supported upfront by your staff. If the need for change is not wholly endorsed, your future success will be limited and compromised.

Some transformational leaders are not always best suited to execute their plans. Thus, implementation of the final vision created may need the assistance of more detailed-oriented managers. This is also useful if the leader's presence is not always highly visible. I have successfully used this style while turning around and reengineering a few of my organizations upon arrival.

Visionary

This approach of "selling, not telling" focuses the movement of staff toward a shared dream. It is all about the "why." The leader's empathy and credibility matter the most here and a collaborative effort is deployed.

Once the leader's vision is clear, the team is empowered to figure out how can they get there (the mission), guided by the leader as to what matters most and why. Staff skill-set development is highly recommended when delivering a new mission statement.

This style is most effective when a clear corporate direction is not known but dearly needed. To be ultimately successful, the leader needs to exhibit strong leadership and management skills simultaneously. I find this style invigorating and have successfully utilized it in combination with the transformational and participative management styles.

Coaching

Coaches connect people's wants and desires with organizational skills to improve performance. Delegating, establishing long-term staff capabilities, addressing career aspirations, giving challenging assignments and stretch targets are useful "to-dos" when incorporating this leadership style.

I thoroughly enjoy coaching, but this activity can be very time consuming. It should not be a leader's full-time job, as much more needs to be accomplished. Plus, you are always limited by how many staff you can coach "one-on-one." This may lead to some resentment from others not as fortunate to gain access to your time. You also need to avoid getting so much into the "weeds" that you lose sight of the big picture of leading your overall organization. The bottom line is I wholeheartedly support coaching as a limited, part-time task but not as a separate leadership style on its own. I have never witnessed this style in full-time application.

Affiliative

This style involves creating harmony and collaboration by connecting people within your team. It is very useful to heal rifts between colleagues, eliminate obstacles, and motivate others during stressful times. This style is typically applied on a more short-term, "as needed" basis. If you periodically use this style, ensure you do not become known as the "peacemaker" who addresses everyone's problems. Otherwise, you can easily become anointed as "head of the corporate daycare center" for adults.

The key here is to find a balance between offering your unbiased input and assistance in addressing issues or roadblocks where necessary to resolve disagreements, while remaining business professionals. Do not avoid addressing performance-related issues as well. It can be a fine line to walk, but it is possible.

Due to my problem-solving nature, I have utilized this style in the past. While useful at times, it has also backfired on me many times when my staff would make a beeline to my door to tell on others or have me address their disagreements before exhausting all other avenues.

Pacesetting

This leadership style involves setting challenging, exciting, and aspirational goals. It works well if your team is talented, motivated, and well experienced. In other words, avoid this style when your team is underdeveloped or lacks self-confidence.

With this style, as the performance standards are set very high and targets are tough to achieve, always doing things faster and better may run the risk of poisoning the work environment and demotivating some of your team. Staff stress and burnout can be common by-products of this style. Utilizing the SMART goalsetting criteria may assist you. SMART is an acronym for (Specific, Measurable, Additive, Realistic, and Timebound). [7]

I used this style a lot earlier in my career and eventually backed away from it. Over time, I continuously heard "all that matters to me is financial results," meaning my colleagues perceived people are secondary to me. Not a position you want to be in, if you believe you are a caring leader. I also had to learn and understand that not everyone is "wired" the same way or as highly motivated as I am to overachieve results. Once I accepted this reality, my team and I lived in better harmony.

Commanding

The commanding style is akin to the autocratic, but this leader does not separate or distance themselves from their followers and are less task oriented. The commanding style's main usage should be dictating a clear direction in times of crisis or emergencies. Winston Churchill, John F. Kennedy, and Steve Jobs have been labeled within this style due to their powerful speeches to inspire their followers and demand expectations. Yet, they possessed transformational qualities as well. This style may also be utilized to kick start a turnaround or deal with problem staff as it's very focused on results.

The commanding style has a negative connotation with many people. To lessen such negativity, this style requires the leader's use of self-control in dealing with their own emotions. Misuse of this style can obviously have negative effects on staff if still in use once the crisis has ended. I have only used this style when I had no other choice, mainly in addressing unprofessional, uncooperative individuals whose behaviors were harming others.

Of these many leadership styles presented, I have used many of them, some with more success than others. Most adaptive leaders also utilize a number of these styles within their repertoire. For example, combining the styles of Visionary, Affiliative, Coaching, and Participative can be very useful in team building and developing your staff. Having this agility is very useful, but be very clear to yourself as to why each style might be implemented as well as its expected benefits and potential negative consequences (e.g., Pacesetter, Commanding).

Changing styles may also cause confusion with staff as they may not be totally sure as to where you are coming from. Staff should be able to "read" you to a certain extent. This allows them to gain an understanding of how you may respond to given situations. Continuous surprises are not usually welcomed. Staying attuned to what truly matters to your staff and articulating a plan as to what is needed and expected of them should resonate more. This should make your selection of various styles to implement less surprising, challenging and acceptable to your team.

Keep in mind that your "soft skills" and personal habits, in addition to technical and on-the-job knowledge, will also assist you in successfully implementing your various combinations of styles. These include being a solid communicator (i.e., speaker, writer, listener, and nonverbal observer), possessing problem-solving skills (e.g., creativity, critical thinking, decision-making, resourcefulness), exhibiting creativity (i.e., curiosity, open-mindedness, innovation), and being adaptive (e.g., optimistic, enthusiastic, flexible, cooperative, patient). These will put a nice "bow" on any of your chosen leadership styles. On the flip side, certain traits and habits will hinder whatever leadership style you choose. These include a lack of presence, direction, transparency, and listening, also, being reactive vs. proactive, unreasonably optimistic (naive), controlling, distant, and narcissistic.

Lessons Learned

I consider myself to be adaptive. Therefore, I refer to my chosen leadership style as "Situational." This is a commonly used style due to its flexibility. As mentioned, I have utilized many if not all the leadership styles; however, some of the more extreme styles were used only very briefly. The selection was based solely on a number of critical factors affecting each of my organizations, the staff as well as the timeline and urgency that must be successfully addressed.

If leaders are not flexible in how they lead based on changing external and internal dynamics, their sustained chances of long-term success may become limited at some point.

Lessons Learned

An analogy I have often shared with my teams to make the point that leaders must be flexible and adaptable is: "You cannot successfully take an old map into a new territory." In other words, navigating with a map of a highway road system of one state or country will not work once you cross the border. Said another way, if you continuously look to the past for future success, you may become history.

What are your thoughts?

What is the leadership style of your current boss, and is it effective?

What is your most effective leadership style and do your colleagues, friends, and loved ones agree?

Is there one new style you want to utilize (which one, why, and in what situation)?

Do you put the needs of your organization, your team, and your family above your own?

CHAPTER 3

Leadership Attributes

Chapter Preview

- **Which personal attributes, traits, and aptitudes are shared by effective leaders**
- **How to utilize storytelling through creating your "teachable point of view"**
- **The importance of mastering Emotional and Cultural Intelligence in your personal and professional lives.**
- **Why "adaptability" is a critical element for continued success**

In the prior chapter, I introduced the various styles that leaders may choose from. A chosen style sets some leaders apart from others' approaches in how they act related to a particular situation. You will recall that each style is distinct but can be combined.

Successful leaders share a common set of attributes no matter which style they practice. These attributes are distinguishable features, qualities, or characteristics that most leaders share.n You either possess them or you do not. Some can be learned, such as emotional intelligence, while others are not so easy to gain. For example, can you teach someone to be humble, charismatic, humorous, empathic, or trustworthy?

These inherent attributes, also referred to as personal traits, cover a wide spectrum of qualitative individual behaviors. When utilized successfully, they become a leader's strengths. These attributes are always present and usually do not change; they are not adapted based on given situations. They are a key part of a leader's "social fabric."

Some of the most distinctive personal traits attributed to successful leaders that I try to utilize include:

Communication

The importance of effective communication is paramount for a leader. A combination of style, methods, frequency, and messaging are all aspects to consider. In general, an individual's method of communicating can be broken down as follows: 7 percent is by actual words, 38 percent by tone of voice, and 55 percent by body language. [8] While these percentages are still under debate, they show how important communication is "beyond the words."

Delivering consistent messages is crucial and prevents unnecessary staff confusion. Communication should be a "two-way street," meaning while you provide and share information, you should also seek feedback and listen openly. This process involves patience, openness, and a desire to seek mutual understanding.

Empathetic listeners not only listen with their ears, but with their mind and heart as well. Leaders should first seek to understand and then to be understood. Be straightforward and transparent when dealing with difficult issues. Always stay calm and under control. Try not to interrupt others.

Communication is about creating an experience for your audience. There should be an effective "give and take." A highly successful communication method to reach your audience is through "storytelling." Sharing your own "Teachable Point of View" (TPOV) is a valuable technique of storytelling created by Noel Tichy. [9]

By utilizing your TPOV, as a communicator, you provide actual examples and experiences that made you the person you are today and is the foundation that drives how you think and operate. Such an approach also shapes how others think of you. Research has shown that storytelling is more effective as a unique learning experience with audiences than sharing your own accomplishments.

Key elements to weave into your stories include your ideals, values, emotions, energy, and edge. Explaining how you take risks and make decisions is also important to articulate.

I learned a proven process of sharing my TPOV through numerous hands-on workshops by one of my organization's multi-year partnerships with Brimstone Consulting. [10] You chart your own personal and professional story (or journey line) right in front of your audience. These details can be mapped out by writing on a simple flip chart or board. The chart should include two axes:

> **Lessons Learned**
>
> Most audiences are motivated by hearing a positive spin of the future: "If we achieve X, good things like Y will occur." Yet, others gain their motivation from a more negative tone: "If we do not achieve X, the future Y may become unclear or problematic." This second form of messaging is known as establishing Fear, Uncertainty, and Doubt (i.e., the FUD factor). I personally prefer the more positive spin. Combining both approaches may allow you to reach more diverse audiences.

- The vertical axis details events from the highs and lows of your life path.
- The horizontal axis lays out a timeline of your journey.
- Key questions to elaborate upon about your journey are:
- Who has influenced your life?
- What have you accomplished and what is next?

- What core values guide you?
- How do you motivate others?
- What should your team expect from you?
- What are your expectations of your team?

The key is to "walk the talk" by use of examples, as this discussion becomes your TPOV. Keep in mind, your TPOV never ends, as it is a lifelong journey. Your capacity to continue learning and adapting your life and career goals should be never ending. Your TPOV is a continuous process, making updates to it as more time passes, and new experiences (with their respective highs and lows) will result.

To truly articulate your TPOV, you need to put your personal guard down and be willing to share your past mistakes, family crises, and other vulnerabilities. You cannot appreciate the mountain peaks unless you have walked through the valleys below. Sharing both types of personal stories will bring you closer to your colleagues, as

Lessons Learned

When communicating, exhibit a willingness and openness to receive bad news. Otherwise, you might only hear what your colleagues think you want to hear as opposed to what you truly need to know. Occasionally and after something went wrong in my organizations, a few of my colleagues would tell me after the fact that they saw it coming. Maybe if they would have been more comfortable in our relationship, we might have prevented or avoided such bad situations.

Lessons Learned

When used appropriately, humor may also lead to gaining financial concessions during heated negotiations. Individuals tend to put down their guard when laughing and enjoying themselves.

they will see you are human too. I have done so and found the experience uncomfortable, but personally liberating. Exude confidence, but not your ego, when sharing your journey.

Humor

If used appropriately and when the time is right, humor can be a useful "ice breaker" to reduce the stress and anxiety of your team or in certain individuals. Try not to make your humor personal or make someone look foolish in front of others. A happier home and work environment is much more enjoyable and can spark greater productivity.

> **Lessons Learned**
>
> The safest humor tactic is to make fun of yourself. Also, be aware that those who play the most jokes in your organization may have the thinnest skin and do not always take kindly to being the brunt of others' jokes.

Humility

"Humility is the awareness that there's a lot you don't know and that a lot of what you think you know is distorted or wrong." [11] While you may become more knowledgeable from others' knowledge, you rarely become wiser from others' wisdom. Humility leads you to wisdom. Be self-confident, but not egotistical. There is usually no need to have to continually prove your worth. Actions speak louder than words. Let others carry your flag and avoid self-promotion.

> **Lessons Learned**
>
> People tend to avoid those individuals who claim they have all the answers. The less someone knows, the more inquisitive and knowledgeable they can become. Remember, there is still a lot you do not know.

Take blame and give credit. Admitting your mistakes makes

Lessons Learned

Once, I was giving a presentation to the majority of my organization. Trying to be humorous, I made what I believed to be an inoffensive comment about a longtime colleague who had just departed our organization. I put my foot in my mouth and the whole room gasped. I dearly wished I could take it back, but the damage was done. I do not believe, from that point forward, anyone paid attention to the rest of my presentation, nor was my heart in it. Afterward, people avoided me, not knowing what to say to me. I stewed over this situation all night. Fortunately, I kicked off the first session the next morning. In front of the same colleagues, I bared it all. I sincerely apologized for my poor taste, as I also held my former colleague and friend in great esteem. My colleagues applauded my admitted mistake. Many came up to me afterward and said how proud they were of me for "righting my wrong." I say, when in doubt, "eat crow or humble pie." You will sleep better.

you a better person, and asking for forgiveness is not a sign of weakness. In fact, others will see you as stronger. Reward shared victories. Winning and celebrating on your own is not as much fun as sharing with others.

Character

As the ancient Greek philosopher Heraclitus of Ephesus stated, "A man's character is his fate." Your character dictates how you choose to live life. This attribute embodies certain moral qualities and logic as to your sense of right and wrong. As a leader, you should be more concerned about your character than your reputation. Your character is about who you are, while your reputation is about what others think you are. Judge others by their worth, not just their abilities.

It might sound counterintuitive, but success can lead to your greatest failure, which is pride. Pride comes from the happiness of your accomplishments and should not be used to measure your worth or that of others. Pride can blind us to reality. Failure, on the other hand, teaches humility and may lead to your greatest future successes. [11] As the legendary UCLA basketball coach John Wooden stated, "While winning does take talent, repeating success takes character." [12]

Possessing compassion for others is another great aspect of character. Avoid being selfish, greedy, and deceptive at all costs. People rarely forget such ill behaviors. Having self-respect is a better mindset. It is not the same as being self-confident, as the former is produced by inner triumphs.

As John Wooden also thoughtfully and masterfully stated: "Talent is God-given... be humble. Fame is man-given... be grateful. Conceit is self-given... be careful." [12]

When you do a good deed for someone, are you disappointed if they do not say thank you? How about when you open a door for a stranger and they just walk through, not even looking at you or saying anything? Do you feel frustrated or unappreciated? If so, I imagine you are not alone. However, you should ask yourself why you did such a nice thing. Hopefully, not for the accolades or a "pat on the back." I sometimes still struggle with this. I should be doing good deeds for the benefit of others, not for my self-gratification.

> **Lessons Learned**
>
> Of all the emotional signals you can exhibit, a smile is the most contagious. And it is much easier on the face muscles than a frown!

Emotional Quotient (EI) vs. Intelligence Quotient (IQ)

Being smart is a good thing, but being wise is better! Being "street smart" is possessing real-world experience through prior actions and interactions. Being "book smart," through academic and theoretical experiences alone, may limit one's ability to weigh all viable business opportunities and threats due to a lack of real-world experience

Possessing both attributes is a winning combination.

It has been well documented that a person's IQ is set at a young age (in their teens) and rarely improves. Intelligence is still very important, but there are some high-IQ people who focus too much time on competitive debate and academic showmanship.

On the contrary, emotional intelligence (EI) can continue to improve over the span of a lifetime. EI can be learned, but it takes a serious commitment. Leaders who possess high EI (the necessary soft skills) successfully build resonant relationships by being in tune with those around them and caring about them. Managing your feelings and your awareness of the feelings of others can also be learned.

Exhibiting compassion is central to EI. Compassion is a deep understanding, concern, and willingness to act for the benefit of others. This is empathy and caring put into action. It is your social candor. Do not confuse empathy with sympathy, however, as the latter is about feeling sorry for someone.

According to Goleman, Boyatis, and McKee, [13] there are four domains to EI:

- **Self-awareness**—Knowing yourself, your strengths and weaknesses, and possessing self-confidence.

- **Self-management**—Having self-control, possessing honesty and integrity, and being adaptive. Can you control your emotions at all times? Out-of-control emotions can make smart people silly.

- **Social awareness**—Showing empathy, having a passion to serve others, and having a sincere interest in the well-being of others.

- **Relationship management**—Making sincere efforts to guide, motivate, and develop others, managing conflicts, making collaboration, and building team. Your personal and professional networks are your future capital.

The first two EI domains are about understanding and managing yourself and your emotions, while the second two are about understanding and managing the emotions of and relationships with others. It is important to note that you cannot achieve success in the last two domains if you have not mastered the first two.

Organizations that possess a strong and visible EI climate exhibit the following common traits:

- Balance between the human and financial sides of the organization
- Organizational commitment to a strategy understood by all
- Active initiatives to improve performance
- Open communication and trust
- Collaboration and resource sharing
- Innovation, calculated risk-taking, and shared learning
- Passion for competition and continuous improvement

A leader without EI may run the risk of inadvertently lowering team or individual morale and performance though employee work overload, a lack of on-the-job autonomy, micromanaging, skimpy rewards provision, unfair treatment, a mismatch creation between the staff's personal values and the demands of their job, and solution of people problems with technological or structural changes instead of being people focused.

EI starts with truly understanding who you are as a person (e.g., awareness of your inner self). If you cannot understand yourself, how on earth do you think you can relate to and understand others?

Lessons Learned

One of my former organizations offered high-end, sophisticated financial modeling to investment analysts. I tried an experiment and recruited a well-schooled and highly intelligent former financial analyst in a sales role. My hope was that he would be able to easily speak the financial language and gain quick credibility that was necessary to close large six-to-seven-figure contracts. While he was able to get us in the door and did speak the language that impressed our prospects, he would get caught up in "tit for tat" debates about which tools were the best and why, as well as how good he was in his former role. The discussion was all about him. My colleague took zero interest in the prospective buyers, never asked them one question, or closed a deal. He exhibited few EI skills. Needless to say, he quickly went back to where he truly belonged, telling other salesmen how smart he was.

Perfecting the following capabilities and competencies (beyond self-awareness) will pay big dividends toward improving your EI: social awareness, empathy and compassion, self-control, conscientiousness, conflict management, adaptability, and relationship management.

Cultural Intelligence

The ability to collaborate with people who process things and act differently from you is a useful

Lessons Learned

My experience has shown that approximately three out of four of my own staff turnover (those who left voluntarily or involuntarily) was related to a lack of EI skills (not being able to or wanting to get along with their peers), rather than a lack of functional expertise or skill set gaps. Also, remember to not confuse passion (positive thinking) with emotion (negative and personal outbursts). The first is controllable; the second is usually not.

> **Lessons Learned**
>
> Ideally, you should surround yourself with colleagues who possess both IQ and EI (mind and heart). But, if I were to choose one over the other, I fall on the side of EI (winning over the heart). Passion, drive, desire, perseverance, persistence, commitment, and loyalty (just to name a few) go a long way toward achieving greater success.

> **Lessons Learned**
>
> I have always tried to ensure I am never the smartest person in the room or meeting. If you were a total stranger and sat in one of my meetings, you should have a difficult time identifying who is truly the overall leader. I prefer to get the job done without running the show.

trait to possess. If developed adequately, this keen awareness allows you to gain a deeper understanding of intercultural complexities through personal encounters with the aim to improve their outcomes.

Elisabeth Plum, [14] who has researched and written extensively on this topic, suggests that cultural intelligence (CI) is a social competence evaluated by the outcome of each encounter. Therefore, it cannot be measured (unlike to an IQ test), as it regularly changes based on the context of each social encounter.

> **Lessons Learned**
>
> The higher you progress within your organization, the greater the importance of EI.

There are three components or dimensions to CI, all of which are equally important and influence each other. These are:

- **Emotion**—A "feeling" component and urge to generate a solution or having an attraction to people who are different. The interest to pursue such an encounter can be driven by external drivers (e.g., a goal or objective needing to be addressed) or internal drivers (e.g., curiosity or attraction). These encounters can end positively or negatively.

- **Understanding**—This is the "cognitive" or "rational" component based on reasoning and making judgments. There is a given and apparent understanding that differences exist between ourselves and others who come from different cultural backgrounds. This component requires knowledge about what culture is and the characteristics that make us different.

> **Lessons Learned**
>
> I learned the importance of CI the hard way, by making various mistakes as I traveled the world with my colleagues. My local colleagues were gracious enough to point out my mishaps in post-mortem meetings. I soon learned to recognize these "faux pas" myself and decided to get involved in a leadership training program. It was a great experience. Since then, I have fewer mishaps and put my local teams in fewer awkward situations. Some of the greatest personal and business experiences I have enjoyed in my career are getting to know so many wonderful people and friends of different cultures.

- **Action**—Brings the other two dimensions into play. This involves the "practical outcome" of what occurred during the encounter (through activities and communication). Various types of interpersonal communications can be exhibited, such as listening, questioning, agreeing, or disagreeing. Other non-verbal communication and techniques of relationship management can also come into play.

Charisma

This is one of the most important traits of a successful leader. It is about one's ability to attract, inspire, and influence others by natural charm and caring. Are you approachable, friendly, and sincere? Can you foster teamwork and a collaborative work environment? Those who possess these traits build stronger teams of loyal followers and believers. It is important that everyone in your organization be treated equally, no matter their position or experience level.

> **Lessons Learned**
>
> I believe charisma is innate. You are born with it and it is not easily taught in school. I would take the power of charisma over position power to influence the actions of others on every occasion. Does your team support you due to their belief in you and your innovative ideas or because you conduct their annual performance review and decide their compensation?

Integrity

Put your colleagues and team above your own issues and needs. Take responsibility for your past actions, admit your mistakes, and fix them. Always keep your word. Exhibit transparency and honesty even if the truth is painful. Be genuine and true to yourself. Never stray from your moral compass. This involves taking the "right" ethical stand on issues, even if they seem unpopular.

When your integrity is being second-guessed, you may never know, as most colleagues will not tell you. People do not always care about how much you know, but more about how much you care.

As our business world continues to evolve and change, future leaders will need to better adapt their skills and personal attributes to include being

> **Lessons Learned**
>
> Regularly asking your colleagues about their family life (without being intrusive) shows you care. Knowing names, ages, hobbies, and upcoming events of their spouses and children goes a long way. Take notes, if need be, to help your memory. Showing empathy truly matters.

> **Lessons Learned**
>
> I strongly believe, as a leader, that your priorities should be centered on the organization first, your colleagues second, and yourself last. Many leaders have these priorities out of order or backwards, and their teams witness such. If this perception exists, they will continue to second-guess your ulterior motives as to whose best interests you have in mind.

> **Lessons Learned**
>
> Sometimes you can learn from other people's mistakes as to "what not to do." I once witnessed one of my bosses ask a colleague about how her gravely ill sister was doing. A very nice and empathic gesture that was well received by her. She smiled, yet before she could respond, his quick follow-up question was "When can I expect that report you're working on for me?" This killed a "caring moment," as surprise and displeasure was written all over her face. Timing is everything.

a change catalyst, having high integrity and honesty, taking a global perspective, leveraging diversity, flexibility, adaptability, open-mindedness, strong communication skills, team building, conflict management, mastery of technology, and a better balance of work/family life.

Conscientiousness

Deliver on your commitments, keep your promises, and be accountable for results. Be punctual, careful, and self-disciplined. Befriend your colleagues. Make sincere efforts to go beyond business issues and learn more about what every individual on your team wants to achieve in their lives (e.g., personal ambitions, family goals, travel, financial security). A balance of personal and professional life is a winning combination and can add to a healthy and motivated workforce. I have found that being happy at home can lead to more productivity at work.

Lessons Learned

One of my former organizations implemented a corporate-sponsored reward program that allowed everyone in the organization to earn a modest bonus if we overachieved our financial results. Everyone bought into the plan and were very excited and supportive to do their part.

We tracked our progress during organization-wide monthly meetings. The room was always at full capacity and we eventually met our targets! I called our group president before our final staff meeting to ensure he was okay with me sharing this great news with my management team first and then with our whole staff. He agreed. So, I did.

We were planning a big year-end celebration when my boss frantically called me, saying to not alert my team, as our global corporate finance department had revised the cashflow results lower. This change dropped us below the stretch target for this key financial metric. Thus, we would now miss out on our bonuses.

My boss instructed me to go back (after I had already shared the good news) and alert my team that due to the revision, we no longer qualified. I did so by alerting my direct reports only. They were quite disappointed and asked me if I believed in this corporate decision.

I thought long and hard about how to respond, as I did not support it at all. Here was my dilemma: If I said I agreed with it, they would have supported me, but I would have lost their trust and respect. If I said I did not agree, I would be going against my parent company's policy, which is generally not appropriate for a leader to do.

I chose to tell my team that I did not support it, then called my boss requesting he come and deliver this news to my organization himself. He did not take me up on my offer to visit us. Instead, he decided to leave the bonus payments as originally calculated. Everyone was paid what they had earned.

This situation brought my team and me closer together, but unfortunately, I lost a tremendous amount of respect for my boss and parent company. I soon voluntarily left this organization. *(continued)*

> Practically every member of my former management team called me (unsolicited) when I joined my new organization, asking me if I had a role for them. I thanked each of them, stating it would not be professional for me as their former CEO to poach them. I still remained loyal to my former organization that had supported me in building my great team over the years. I was proud to have left it in a better state than I had found it in.

I hate to end this hopefully inspiring section on a bad note, but let's quickly summarize some of the less positive leadership traits you should try to avoid. Please do not pass blame, fail to give credit, avoid conflicts, micromanage, or get too deep in the trenches. Avoid showing a lack of ambition and ownership. Do not try to rationalize poor or unethical conduct. Do not neglect or forget to focus on your own self-development and personal growth.

What are your thoughts?

What are the most important attributes a leader should possess?

Do you share these in common with both your personal and professional life?

Are there certain attributes you can improve or add (why)?

Do you utilize storytelling and your TPOV to successfully communicate?

Map out your TPOV journey line and test it with others closest to you. Did it bring you even closer together as to their greater understanding as to who you are?

Have you successfully mastered the EI domains of self-awareness and self- management? If yes, how about social awareness and relationship management?

What does cultural awareness and sensitivity mean to you? Do you consider your work team and friends culturally diverse?

CHAPTER 4

Leadership Work Environment

Chapter Preview

- Key steps to create a safe, healthy, and enjoyable work environment.

- Key components necessary to create effective Vision and Mission statements and to avoid pitfalls.

- Critical questions to address when transforming a stagnant organization.

- The distinguishing characteristics of a successful coach and mentor.

- Why succession planning is important yet difficult to achieve

- Benefits that cultural and skill set diversity can bring to your organization.

Many researchers state that motivation comes from within individuals. What is important to them and what tends to motivate them changes and shifts over time as they age, mature, and gain more experience in life. I support this premise.

The leader's role is to establish a healthy and motivational work environment that enables a positive workspace, while eliminating negative forces and barriers. These are the ideal conditions for staff self-motivation to occur.

Start by developing your people. They are your greatest asset. They should come first and be your top priority. The organization's numbers (financial performance) should follow as a close second. If your team believes financial results are all that matter, they may quickly lose interest in them and believe their own well-being and future development no longer matter. There is a direct cause-and-effect relationship taking place in this scenario that I have personally witnessed.

Remember, you work for your staff and if they succeed, you succeed. I continuously preached this to all my teams. Interestingly, it takes a lot of time for everyone to believe you, no matter how sincere you are being. As a leader, you can rarely do everything on your own, particularly as you continue to climb the corporate ladder.

Establishing a realistic "work/life balance" is essential for you and your team to stay healthy and to recharge. This includes ensuring your team takes their deserved time off (e.g., personal leaves, vacations, holidays). At times, you may have to insist a few colleagues take their allotted time off. In rare situations, I instructed colleagues to provide me with their quarterly schedule to allow them adequate time to plan and take days or weeks off. Recharging themselves is in the employees' and organization's best interests.

As a leader, look to your future "stars" (the top performers on your team who offer the greatest growth potential). They should be easy to

> **Lessons Learned**
>
> Everyone within your team should be treated fairly, equitably, professionally, and consistently. Beware of showing personal favoritism, as this can be seen negatively by others. However, your best and brightest employees (your "stars") deserve extra attention, beyond the norm. The 80/20 rule applies here, as a minority of your team probably delivers 80 percent of the results. How can you move others into this 20 percent?

identify from a qualitative standpoint as they should exhibit competencies such as influence, team leadership, organizational awareness, self-confidence, a drive to achieve, and overall leadership skills.

Establishing inspirational Vision and Mission Statements are enablers in building a stronger work environment, as they enable a clearer path to a successful future. Leaders should understand what issues and needs are universally shared among their colleagues. Then, capitalize on and tap into these to map out a better future.

If your team does not believe in your Vision and Mission, they will never come to fruition. Per George F. Will, "The future has a way of arriving unannounced." Be prepared to seize the moment to ensure your collective future is understood and embraced.

Vision

If you have no vision, you will have no direction. As Charles Lutwidge Dodgson (pen name Lewis Carroll) said, "If you don't know where you are going, any road will get you there." But then again, how will you know when you have arrived? The same goes for organizations. Creating a Vision Statement for the future requires a tremendous amount of effort on both the leader's and the team's part, as this is a collaborative effort.

A Vision Statement should be clear, lucid, and coherent and should present an inspirational and meaningful picture of your future direction. In a nutshell, it provides hope and the reason for your organization's being. As Oscar Wilde (Irish poet and play writer) stated, "To stop dreaming is to give up on hope. To stop hoping is to give up on dreams."

When creating a Vision Statement, keep it simple yet compelling and inspirational. It is important that the leader not provide all the answers but instead ask the right questions to spark passionate discussions. I find asking broad questions useful, such as:

- Why do we exist?
- Where do we want to go and why?
- What are we trying to accomplish?
- What are we committing to do and why?
- How will we become unique, add value, and create a competitive advantage?

Statistics have shown that successfully creating a clear and embraced Vision Statement improves stakeholder satisfaction levels and can drive a significant uptick in related benefits compared to organizations who fail at this task. A clear Vision Statement clarifies your purpose, creates a sense of belonging and a shared identity, and sets the context and tone of your organizational climate.

> **Lessons Learned**
>
> Upon joining all my organizations, one of my first mandates was to refresh or create completely new Vision and Mission Statements. A new "Transformational" or "Visionary" leader is usually not brought in unless the organization has somehow lost its way and is underperforming as a result. If we were to become more relevant and successful, a major transformation was warranted. Thus, we needed to reinvent ourselves.

Mission

Once your vision is set, the next step is to articulate how you plan to "win" by delivering it. How will you execute it through the best and most efficient course of "prioritized" actions? Your Mission Statement is more about today, while your Vision Statement is about tomorrow.

Your Mission Statement should focus on what your organization does and how it does so by various means and why. Being innovative in delivering your mission should not be left out. Lastly, your Mission Statement should address and articulate your organizational culture, ethics, values, and behaviors through which your goals are delivered.

Once the Vision, "the why," is clear, I proceed to how and what. New Vision and Mission Statements are underpinned by stating a "Case for Change." If my new teams did not see the need for, and understand and support such an undertaking, we were all wasting our time. This starts with taking a serious and brutally honest view of where we are today.

In most instances, these negative aspects were the same in all my organizations:

- A lack of strong and visible leadership.
- Much of the people talent had departed and overall morale was low.
- No clear strategy or strong value proposition was in place.
- Financial performance was on a steady decline.
- Market positions were saturated with products in stagnant growth or serious decline, needing to be discontinued or reinvigorated.

> **Lessons Learned**
>
> Both Vision and Mission Statements are not written in stone. They will and should evolve and possibly be revised over time based on internal and external changes and new challenges. They can be viewed as a work in progress.

> **Lessons Learned**
>
> Avoid long preambles for your Vision. If the Vision and Mission cannot be stated in one or two simple sentences, it's probably too long, too complex, and few will understand or embrace it. I have personally witnessed Vision and Mission statements that were so long, the only way to repeat them was through memorization. These had long lost their meaning to staff. Rarely are these fully embraced either.

- The product portfolios were old, outdated, and lacked true innovation.
- Technology investments were almost nonexistent or poorly spent.

It was usually quite easy to gain consensus and agree that if serious and robust change did not occur soon, "the end was near." Our challenge was to decide and address the "why, what, how, and by when."

For a commercial organization, the "what" is clear (profitable and sustainable growth). The "how" is achieved by creating greater value. How will you separate your organization from the rest through a unique market positioning? Creating unique value leads to profits. One feeds the other. Common business levers (e.g., activities and initiatives) that have significant mid- to long-term top-line growth potential are driven by developing new, relevant products and penetration into new markets and diversification.

All my organizations had typically been taking a very narrow view of the markets in which we competed and the products we offered to them. We challenged this premise with much success as to where expansion could occur and how. We focused on and addressed a few key questions, such as:

- In what markets do we compete and what are the specific sector dynamics? Are these sustainable in long term and do we still want to compete here?
- Are there other markets into which we could expand and what would it take?
- What would be our compelling competitive advantage and value proposition in doing so (where, how, and why)?
- What does our ultimate future success look like, both from a quantitative and qualitative perspective?

- How will we measure success and under what timelines?
- What type of organizational structure and resources are best suited to support our efforts?
- Do we need to enhance our current competencies and capabilities? If so, what is needed and where?

As you can imagine, much thought and effort went into elaborating these questions and other related issues. All my organizations were eventually turned around and began delivering consistent, healthy growth.

Here are a few successful highlights and outcomes of our efforts from a few industry sectors:

- **Publishing**—Shifting from just printing undergraduate textbooks and expanding into the broader education realm while moving up the value chain. We expanded our market reach and pursued continuous/adult learning, vocational/technical, community college, graduate-level content, training, driving curriculum change by adding soft-side skills, online distribution of content, data, tools and apps, testing, assessment and certification, remedial education, and AI testing for online tutoring, just to name a few.

- **Financial Institutions**—Expanding beyond our existing base of serving community and commercial banks into the insurance and investment banking sectors with a product focus on data analytics and regulatory compliance.

- **Aviation**—Expanding beyond just serving airlines into serving all Travel and Tourism market segments (i.e., the industry's total value and supply chain), including hotels, car rental, ride sharing, cruise, etc. We also expanded our user bases to include other forms of multimodal transport, financial institutions, hospitals, universities, technology, logistics, and distributors who had business or commercial ties and/or interest in aviation. These non-airline segments became our fastest growing markets as we achieved maximum diversification and market reach. Our new product portfolios were focused on new data and predictive analytics, corporate training, certification and assessment, blended learning, smart interactive, digital publishing, and end-to-end integrated solutions (e.g., packaging data, training, and consulting services into one service offering).

In summary, it is very possible to turn a lagging organization around, if you focus first on its people and reengage them with a compelling vision of a bright future that they agree on and take ownership of to deliver themselves.

Coaching and Mentoring

Coaching is a form of developmental activity with a shorter term of completion. Coaching can take the form of face-to-face or virtual meetings depending on the location of the coach and learner. Coaching is more focused and structured for the learner to achieve specific, agreed-upon personal and professional goals within a finite duration. The coach may incorporate a myriad of techniques from "hands-on" training, instruction, guidance, action plans, and advice related to the learner's specific tasks and objectives. The goal or outcome is usually for the learner to achieve greater performance results.

Coaching takes a great deal of patience and mutual trust between the coach and learner. Coaches may utilize a variety of styles, including directive (one-way communication), cooperative (two-way dialogue), or a causal, informal, "on the fly" approach.

A key trait of a good coach is being nonjudgmental, while offering constructive criticism to correct issues without creating learner resentment. Other traits of a "quality" coach include being self-aware, listening well, being well prepared, understanding the learner's strengths and weaknesses, being committed to specific solutions, and always having alternate action plans, if needed.

The learner gains numerous benefits from a quality coaching experience, such as better prioritization of their targets, learning to challenge the status quo, gaining a fresh perspective on themselves and their organization, and increased morale.

Mentoring, on the other hand, is different from coaching. Mentoring is a more informal long-term process that usually involves a more senior leader as the mentee's champion. The mentor can be a source of wisdom by offering their experience, knowledge, and expertise as well as by setting developmental goals, providing advice on career growth, opening doors to assist in mentee networking, and developing new contacts for those under their stewardship.

Benefits for the mentee include gaining more confidence, new ideas, and different ways of thinking, developing strategies to improve their strengths, and overcoming their weaknesses, improving interpersonal skills, increasing their visibility and recognition through networking.

Lessons Learned

Over the years, I missed out on many opportunities to seek mentorship for myself. I rarely sought advice and paid little attention when such advice was being offered. My loss. Do not make the same mistake.

I highly recommend, where and when possible, you make yourself available to guide and develop your targeted colleagues and peers, whether as a coach or mentor, if you have the passion and interest, of course. These processes require time and patience, but the long-term benefits for you and those you impact are tremendous.

Lessons Learned

At any given point in time, I am usually coaching or mentoring approximately ten to twelve individuals. The majority of these were women as they sought me out more than men. It was well known that I am a strong supporter of gender diversity and inclusion. A significant percentage of all my management teams (50 percent) consisted of many talented women. Numerous women outside my team regularly sought my guidance and career advice. My advice is simple: never hold back anyone's career ambitions to satisfy your own self-serving motives.

Lessons Learned

Mentoring is not just about passing on the positive attributes of leadership, but also having mentees learn from your own mistakes of what not to do. Allow them to learn from your own successes and failures as to not have them reinvent the wheel. Allowing them to make smaller, less impactful mistakes can also be a learning experience.

Lessons Learned

Everyone should understand their purpose in life. Do you live to work or work to live? Know who you are and who you want to become. What gets your passion and energy flowing and why? This is what life is all about.

Lessons Learned

Coaching others is a continuous, daily on-the-job activity. Most evenings when I arrived home after work, I would quickly assess if I had been able to effectively assist others with some form of lasting effect. If I identified a few, I considered it a good day.

Succession Planning

This type of talent management planning is critical for an organization's long-term sustainability. If people are their most important asset, why do so many organizations neglect to successfully implement a comprehensive succession plan? The simple answer is because it is not easy and there is not just one proven method to deploy.

Successful implementation of succession planning should include agreeing upon the categories (position levels) to include and the timelines for tracking key individuals (e.g., one to three to five years looking outward). This is also predicated on each senior manager's individual situations and career plans as well as those of their team members. This is a fluid, ever-changing, and HIGHLY CONFIDENTIAL process.

As mentioned, the key question that needs to be addressed is what levels (positions) within your organization will be included in the succession plan? With each lower level/layer/band of positions you chose to add, your plan will become exponentially more complex to manage and track.

Deciding how individuals are selected is also critical. Is this a collaborative senior management discussion or do individuals select their own candidates? I highly support a collaborative debate with clear selection criteria and guidelines set. Other important questions to answer include:

- Is how will your team ensure a serious commitment to diversity and inclusion embedded into your selection criteria? How will this be measured?

- What plans will be put in place and what commitments will you make to continue the ongoing development of the selected individuals to ensure their readiness when the time comes?

- How often will these candidates be reviewed or dropped, and others potentially added?

- How will your plan be rolled out and communicated across your organization?

Succession planning is one of the most important staff developmental processes a senior management team should undertake. It needs a lot of time and dedicated attention and should not be coupled with other unrelated topics on your management meeting agenda.

Individually, if you desire to move up within your organization or move on to another organization, the best method is to begin the planning to eventually replace yourself. Many managers and leaders struggle with this premise due to a lack of self-confidence, fearing they may be replaced before moving on to another, better role. But such preparation of a few suitable candidates is essential to your own mobility.

If you are selected for a promotion, the first job you will have is to identify your successor. Be prepared ahead of time or you might find yourself in the situation of doing two jobs or having to put up with a lengthier transition from your current role to the new one. Such delays can be up to six months.

If you do decide to depart your current organization, ensure you leave your team in a better position than it was in when you arrived. Do not burn bridges on your way out. Be polite, gracious, and always professional. One day, you may need them for a quality reference.

One of the biggest challenges related to succession planning is how you communicate your plan to staff and what you say about it. Such messaging should be motivating to all interested staff, while others may unfortunately perceive it as unfair, biased, and only for a few of their "favored" peers.

One way to avoid confusion and frustration is to include succession planning as part of everyone's developmental plan during their performance review process. This provides them confidential one-on-one time to discuss specific career-related issues with their supervisor.

It is also important to not overpromise career growth by alerting someone they are in a select group of possible and future stars. If things do not go as planned, disappointment and unhappiness may occur, and you may have unnecessarily demotivated a top performer. A better approach is to talk to them more about the actions they need to take and by when to ensure they are prepared and ready when opportunity knocks. This is a fine line to walk.

From a healthy work environment perspective, be aware of your colleagues and peers who have narrower views and believe their on-the-job knowledge and know-how is power (e.g., job security). While they may think this to be true, it is not. Everyone is replaceable and post-heroic leadership (our business cannot succeed without me) is old school thinking. A dead giveaway is an unwillingness to share knowledge and teach others. Such actions can become poisonous to the organization if not corrected or stopped.

There is no room in your organization for paranoid, non-team players. It is much better to deal with these culprits sooner rather than later, as they rarely change, nor will the barriers they have created go away. If they continue to get away with disruptive actions and behaviors, as the leader, you will lose credibility for turning a "blind eye" and not addressing them. Ultimately, they hamper speed, productivity, and other team members' morale. Ironically, these individuals are also the ones who continue to shout the loudest, asking, "What is my next career move or promotion and when?" Interestingly, they usually lack self-confidence that their peers do not see.

Cultural Diversity and Inclusion

Culture is the existence of variety within our society. It encompasses a distinct pattern of behaviors, beliefs, and specific characteristics of groups of people. These are passed down from generation to generation and are very difficult to shift. The opposite of a culturally diverse group is a monoculture (one way of thinking and acting), which is quite boring.

Do not try to clone yourself; instead, surround yourself with a team of colleagues that is very different from you in all aspects of business and life experiences. We all obtain stronger results from a wider range of insights and perspectives, and we all have a role to play in creating an inclusive workplace where every colleague can be their authentic self.

Strive for diversity of thoughts and identify those who view complexity from different angles. Leverage differences in gender, race, age, nationality, etc. and ensure everyone has a voice. A recent study showed that organizations with an above-average gender, race, and ethnic diversity mix within their leadership roles are much more likely to perform better in comparison to their top competitors.

> **Lessons Learned**
>
> I have always made the effort to recruit people who are smarter and more knowledgeable than me in key areas where I am not the strongest. Societally, individuals who think and process issues differently than me. If you are always viewed as the smartest person in the room, you are destined to just repeat the past. Understand, appreciate, and respect the differences between cultures.

The following are a few cultural dimensions that are important to recognize, as culture effects our values and values effect our behaviors: [15]

Power Distance is defined as the relationship and extent to which less powerful members of an organization accept and expect unequal power distributions by both the leader and followers. This can be quite different across varying cultures. This cultural dimension involves how comfortable staff are to interact with people they perceive to be higher than them in the organization's hierarchy (e.g., CEO and senior management). Within North America, this power distance is usually narrow, more informal, where staff may even choose to call their CEO by their first name. However, in most Asian cultures, this power distance is much wider and formal. Staff may rarely feel comfortable approaching or questioning the boss.

Uncertainty Avoidance is another cultural dimension to consider. This involves how comfortable colleagues are within their own roles based on their job description and the amount of tolerance they have of unpredictability. There are those who prefer everything spelled out in black and white. Being "boxed in" is a comfort for them, while others prefer their roles to be more grey and less clear, allowing them wiggle room and flexibility to accomplish the job and other tasks as they see fit.

> **Lessons Learned**
>
> Establish a work environment whereby colleagues are comfortable challenging each other's ideas (even the boss). The lone decenter may have the best point or idea. A thousand colleagues supporting a bad idea still remains a bad idea. Beware of territorial behaviors that may be the best option for an individual or their department, but not necessarily for the whole organization.

> **Lessons Learned**
>
> Always challenge culture bias and intolerance. Create a team environment based on collaboration and cooperation as well as shared credit and rewards.

There are other cultural dimensions to consider and understand before deciding how best to lead and communicate with a diverse team. These include individual-collectivism, masculinity-femininity, long-term orientation, and self-restrain. This topic is worth investigating and researching more. [15]

Time, attention, and careful thought should be given to the younger generation of colleagues who have grown up in a much different world than my baby-boomer generation. We are now well into the "selfie" generation where less empathy may exist, and materialism is more prevalent.

Many Gen X and Ys want to be part of an organization that has a real purpose and compelling reason for being. If you cannot appeal to them, their wants, and desires, they will be difficult to attract and retain. This applies to customers from these generations as well.

These younger "up-and-comers" should have a voice in our future and an important place in our organizations. Many correctly challenge the status quo by questioning why we do things as we do. We should listen to them, try to understand their point of view, and learn from them. We should put ourselves in their shoes and appreciate how they may perceive many of us to be "old-timers" wearing "corporate blinders." I recall being one of the youngest in the meeting room and thinking the exact same thing! Adaptability, flexibility, and compromise will win out in the end.

When I informally asked what our younger generational employees want in a leader, the most common answers were that the leader should be a good communicator with strong interpersonal skills and someone who takes initiative. By taking initiative, they mean a leader who is prepared to proactively address events before they occur (preventative maintenance) vs. the one who just reacts to the events with little forethought. Taking initiative without sharing empathy, however, can prove destructive as the consequences to others are not considered. In summary, employees state that their organizational climate is traced back to one individual, their leader.

Recent and more formal studies found that Gen Xers and Gen Ys stated the most important traits that a quality leader should possess are honesty, transparency, and technical competencies. They want a leader who is supportive and committed to their performance and who values their work autonomy and independence. The leadership styles they prefer are pacesetting, coaching, and visionary in this order. [16]

> **Lessons Learned**
>
> When I taught a graduate business course at one of the top ten universities, 70 percent of my class of more than eighty students was of Asian descent. As part of my grading scale, 25 percent of the students' final grade was dictated by individual class participation. Possessing strong verbal communication, debating, and critical-thinking skills are very important attributes in business.
>
> Being naïve at that time and not culturally aware or astute, I would regularly ask the class for their comments and challenges to my lecture. Often, a US student would freely speak up, not raising their hand to be recognized. Then, another US student would do the same, usually just repeating what the other had just stated before.
>
> My Asian students rarely got a word in edgewise. A group of them finally stopped by my office, concerned about this 25 percent of their grade that they saw as "at risk." They shared that, culturally, they were taught not to speak up unless being recognized and were respectfully to never challenge their professors or elders. We agreed on a plan whereby I could call upon them, individually, for their thoughts. They were comfortable with this approach and everything worked out much better.

Skill Set Diversity

Try as you might, you cannot be an expert in every area. As you build your career, you will have two choices as you gain additional expertise and experience:

- Gain knowledge "a mile deep and an inch wide" by becoming a subject matter expert (SME) in one or two areas and possessing little to no knowledge in other functions. Some of these SMEs tend to think they have all the answers, and ask few questions. Future learning may stall as they rarely step out of their comfort zone. They are content with a career ambition of growing vertically within one function.

- Strive for knowledge "a mile wide and an inch deep." Such a "jack of all trades, master of none" is not necessarily seen as an expert in any area, but as having acceptable knowledge of all functions. The key to success here is always asking questions to deepen your knowledge base. You are viewed as a "utility" person who can be asked to take on many different roles and tasks. In times of organizational change, this can be useful for job security, but also important for flexibility with more possible promotion opportunities.

The career dilemma faced by these choices will depend on where you want to go in your career once you move up in an organization to a more senior level (e.g., director, VP). It can be very difficult to move into a totally new function at a higher level with little experience While this is not impossible to accomplish, there are always other leagues vying for the same position who have mastered such knowledge and "know-how." Thus, your chances of attaining the new role are obviously lower. One way to counter this, while time permits, is to make a few horizontal moves (function to function) to gain an understanding of many other roles and functions within your organization. You will have then opened many opportunities for upward mobility in more areas.

Social Responsibility

Make a sincere effort to be socially and environmentally conscious. Rethinking your operational processes or understanding how customers use your products and services in relation to their environmental impacts is a crucial discussion to be undertaken.

Going "green" where possible makes sense. Tracking, reducing and communicating your organization's efforts to go carbon neutral is important as well as aspirational. Such corporate visibility and actions can positively impact your "brand equity" within your community.

Also, participate in, donate to, and allow your colleagues to join local programs to assist your community and/or assist others in need. Act with a human touch. Giving back can be very fulfilling and brings your team members closer together for many good causes beyond making corporate profits.

What are your thoughts?

What are the most important factors in establishing a safe, healthy, and enjoyable work environment?

Is your work/life balance in sync (if not, what needs to change)?

Are your organization's Vision and Mission Statements clear and understood by all the staff (if not, how might such gaps be closed)?

Have you been a coach or mentor to others? If so, was it a mutually rewarding relationship (why)?

Do you currently have a coach or mentor? If not, how might you benefit from each?

Have you identified a few individuals that might become your successor? What are you doing to prepare them?

What efforts do you make to ensure those around you are culturally diverse, are engaged, and have complimentary skill sets?

How can you ensure that all six cultural dimensions are understood and embraced by your colleagues?

CHAPTER 5

Leadership and Strategy

Chapter Preview

- **Why Strategic Intent is so important, and what it provides**

- **A step-by-step approach to creating Strategic and Business Development plans.**

- **The important role Organizational Design plays in the successful execution of your strategies.**

- **Organizational structure types and which organizations are utilizing each.**

It is the leader's responsibility to ensure everyone understands where their business aspires to go, why it should do so, and how it will get there. The "what and how" equates to your mission and includes the means of achieving your vision, the "why," which is your purpose. This messaging will be easy to articulate only if every individual understands exactly how and where their role fits into achieving your strategic intent. They should then be able to successfully support and deliver it.

Strategic Intent

The strategic intent [17] lays out an organizational plan of action to attain your organizational objectives and achieve a predefined future state and organizational vision (purpose). It drives organizational processes to maintain competitive advantage or to seek a new one through change. Its focus should always center on how you will succeed. This process is accomplished by the creation of a strategic roadmap or blueprint of specific initiatives based on available resources and capabilities which becomes the strategic plan.

A strategic plan is developed by way of implementing an official planning process. This process includes the alignment and integration of all related organizational activities and resources. The time horizon for a strategic plan is for longer term (covering three to five years), as most initiatives to be carried out will take more time to deliver compared to short-term annual operational activities.

What makes a successful strategic planning process? Communication is one critical element to ensure the complete participation and alignment at all organizational levels. Such dialogue and interaction between staff should be cross-divisional in nature to secure understanding, commitment, and integration across the whole organization to deliver its strategic goals.

Strategic planning includes three main steps. Each of these steps should occur simultaneously at the upper, middle, and operational levels of your organization to foster stronger communication, idea sharing, and ultimate integration.

Step 1: Strategy Formulation—This is achieved by assessing your organization's current internal situation as well as external market dynamics. This "audit" can be conducted in a short time period. One useful strategic planning technique and tool that has been around for years is the of Swot (strengths, weaknesses, opportunities, threats) analysis, which is used to identify and compare your organization's internal and external positions to those of your competitors. [18]

SWOT analysis is a useful starting point in the strategic planning process. Once completed, you should have a better understanding of where your organization is today as you prepare a plan to reach where you want to go in the future. With the right, knowledgeable staff involved, a SWOT analysis can be constructed in little time via one or more brainstorming sessions.

Step 1 also includes deciding which markets and products/services you will pursue as well as those you may abandon. These plans should spell out operational resource allocations and funding requirements. Seeking outside funds from venture capital/private equity firms as well as merger and acquisition opportunities may be options for consideration.

Step 2: Implementation—Putting a strategic plan into action involves establishing measurable goals, activities, objectives, and targets. These are then supported by designing an appropriate organizational structure, establishing efficient processes, and maximizing resource productivity. Once again, two-way communication is crucial at this step to ensure staff buy-in. Successful execution of a chosen strategy is one of the most important priorities of all leaders.

Step 3: Evaluation—This phase of your strategic planning process is intended to better understand the internal and external factors that are affecting the successful implementation of your plans, both positively and negatively. Performance should be continuously measured, and corrective actions should be taken.

In summary, the culmination of a successful strategic planning process should present a small number of focused and agreed-upon strategies. These should be efficiently executed and delivered by cost-effective activities that produce relevant market-valued outcomes with positive financial results while avoiding undue financial risks.

Benefits of strategic planning include:

- Better strategic focus by using a system-wide approach
- More appropriate resource allocation
- More effective decision-making
- Enhanced communication and ownership of performance at all organizational levels

- Improved staff empowerment and satisfaction through a decentralized process
- Increased chances of goal achievement

Business Development Plan—Many of my organizations have taken an extra step in the strategic planning process by including a business development plan. The purpose of this "financially driven" plan is to propose more details about how and where to integrate all the activities and resources related to the achievement of your strategic intent. The result of this financial plan should indicate an expected financial performance baseline or "base case." This is what you expect to occur if all things go as planned. However, in certain situations, you may want to be more aggressive and request more funding and resourcing to go beyond your "base case." This will require you to create a "best case" financial scenario to justify the additional funding. Obviously, this "best case" plan includes higher revenues, profits, and more risk. Lastly, upper management usually requests a "worst case" financial performance scenario. This more financially conservative or pessimistic view details what might occur if your plan is affected by unavoidable, unexpected external and internal factors.

These three scenarios assist upper management in addressing the possibility of "if we invest X in certain activities, we then expect Y in revenue growth, giving us Z in profits." Each of the three financial cases will have their own costs, revenues, and profits for a final decision to be rendered based on risk tolerance.

The projected financial results of each case are shown on a year-by-year basis, usually over the first three years of the plan period. Going out any further than three years with detailed financial projections can be an effort in futility, as uncertainty increases the further out you go.

I strongly recommend focusing more time on getting the first year correct. The outer years can be calculated by utilizing financial modeling and percentage growth variances. Putting in future financial expectations by the way of "placeholders" for the development of future new products should also be included if pushing projections beyond three years (in years four to five). A placeholder is a generic way of projecting growth from future services planned, but not yet under development or market tested. I tend to take a conservative approach to these by under-promising and eventually (hopefully) overdelivering.

If you eventually miss (underachieve) your Year One performance, all the outer years' expected growth percentages will automatically need to be inflated. This is due to your outer years' financial targets being set upon your Year One baseline.

Projected financial results are critical to any strategic plan as the leader should understand what business activities will be executed at what operational costs, including special investments in particular projects. These costs are then rolled up to correspond to expected revenues and profits.

The business development plan is an iterative give-and-take process, as rarely does the first draft meet the leader's financial expectations. Thus, the team may need to go back to the drawing board several times to revise and tweak their plans to meet the leader's profitability and growth requirements.

To address the dilemma, does the team increase revenues on the same cost basis or lower the costs, keeping projected revenues the same? Or some combination of both? Obviously, each iteration of this revision exercise brings greater risk into the plan. But it should be manageable if the leader's growth expectations are not overly aggressive or unrealistic. This is a fine line for everyone to manage accordingly. Mutual trust and respect are needed between all participants.

Strategic planning does have its flaws and pitfalls. These include:

- Putting a tremendous amount of time and effort into a "paper-driven" exercise, while possibly taking your eyes off current business activities and operations. When dealing with internal issues, you may have your back to the customer.

- Risking that, once the planning is complete, it is "shelved" and never followed up on, updated, or seen again. A strategic plan should not be a static document.

- Targets too ambitious due to the lack of capabilities and competencies to deliver them.

- Having political infighting between departments and divisions as to who gets what.

- Possessing an organizational culture that lacks flexibility and agility.

Lessons Learned

Over the years as a leader, I have experimented with two different approaches to providing guidance to the business development planning process. In the first, I told them that overall projected expense growth can only be half of expected revenue growth. My goal was to protect our future profit margins. However, I did not give them a specific target or percentage of profitable growth expectation. This was my only guidance to them. My team had the freedom to spend more money in the areas that could reap the greatest growth, but were then required to cut back expenses in lower growth areas. It was their call. This empowered them and provided the freedom they needed to construct their own plans with profits they felt were acceptable.

Unfortunately, I quickly learned that this process wasted a lot of time, as the team rarely met my expense/revenue growth ratio percentages on the first "go round." Thus, my second option was to provide them with a more specific, overall expected profit growth target (e.g., +10 percent). This came with clear instructions of "do not come back to me with a lesser number." This still provided them with the ability to manipulate every area within of their plan so long as the bottom line met my overall growth target. I made myself available to discuss challenges they faced during this exercise. This method seemed to work better and was a more efficient use of their time.

Lessons Learned

I have found that, in "good times," many organizations' upper management inadvertently take their eyes off the ball from a strategic perspective. They forget to keep a keen focus on thinking about the longer term and naively focus more on their current successes. They do not give a lot of thought on how such successes will continue. Thus, they tend to sometimes miss reoccurring business cycles and economic fluctuations. Nor do they have contingency plans in place for these and other unplanned occurrences. Who pays the ultimate price for this lack of upper management planning and foresight? Unfortunately, their staff.

In the strategic planning process, there are many issues that need to be considered with new market expansion, including the market's overall attractiveness and growth trends, as well as your willingness to commit the time, effort, and resources necessary to succeed. A few questions to ask yourself include:

- Are new skills and capabilities needed?
- Do you know how you will reach these untapped markets?

- Do you have a keen understanding of the processes you need to successfully adapt to ensure you retain your current competitive advantages?

Of all the new market opportunities, expanding into emerging markets offers the greatest growth potential due to their sheer size, demographics, growth trends, increasing demand for new goods and services, lower labor costs, etc.

> **Lessons Learned**
>
> I am a big supporter of pursuing growth via entering new markets. This strategy, often referred to as "strategic market development," has been a component of every strategic plan with which I have ever been associated.

Overall, my organizations have had mixed success entering such markets. Now, when I think about which markets to enter, beyond the issues I mentioned above, I also ask pointed questions to better understand such issues as:

- Political climate and government's role and policies
- Crime and corruption rates
- Language barriers
- Accepted currencies
- Requirement of partnering with a local vendor

These factors were many of the culprits leading to a few of our past unsuccessful emerging market expansion attempts. A large and growing market may look promising on paper, but if you do not totally understand and appreciate the local dynamics of conducting business there, you may be in for a rude awakening. In my experience, when entering emerging markets, the "how" supersedes the "why."

Organizational Design

Once a strategic intent and plan is created, the next step involves its execution. The execution process includes designing the structure in which your organization will function, operate, and align resources. Organizational design refers to the composition of the organization's units (e.g., divisions, operations, etc.), the positions within each, and the relationships between them. The goal is to identify and design a "fit" between your strategic choices and your organization's structure.

The structure defines how activities, tasks, responsibilities, coordination, and supervision are to be directed to achieve organizational objectives and goals based on the chosen strategies. Whatever structure is chosen, it should be clear as to who makes key decisions at each level. The structure in place is also how staff will view their organization and work environment. The end game here is to align strategies with operations to create an efficient foundation for standard operating procedures (SOPs), maximize flexibility, and drive innovation, while securing a unique competitive advantage.

Most organizations have either a flatter, more horizontal structure with fewer levels of middle management between staff and upper management or a more vertical hierarchical structure with more layers of management. The horizontal model entails that each manager's scope, responsibilities, and number of staff under their guidance is increased. Yet, the overall organization's chain of command is smaller. The goals here are to give managers more autonomy, decentralize staff with greater empowerment, and involve them in decision-making. This situation should create a more collaborative, cross-functional work environment and a culture with less bureaucracy vs. the traditional command-and-control style found with vertical hierarchy structures. However, creating fewer management layers may lead to the need to downsize to keep a realistic supervisory-to-staff ratio, which would have the benefit of lowering costs.

Most larger organizations opt for the more hierarchical vertical design with additional layers of management and related authority. This structure entails that every entity within it is subordinate to another. The only exception is at the top. The communication takes place between each direct supervisor and their subordinates. This results in less organizational communication overload, yet limits information flows as well.

Selection of either a vertical or horizontal design implementation should include addressing and fixing existing dysfunctional or ineffective workflows, processes, systems, and decision-making protocols. Both the technical, operational, and people sides of your organization should benefit from such efficiency measures and barrier removals.

> **Lessons Learned**
>
> Based on my experience with organizational designs, if I had to choose between a "perfect" organizational structure that is "fit for purpose" but lacks some key people talent to deliver it and an organizational design that has some flaws but possesses a quality and talented team, I will always choose the latter. I have found that talented, passionate, and committed people get the desired results no matter what structure they work in. They overcome any barriers they face by creating work-arounds and keeping communication lines open at all times.

Organizational Structure Types

After thoroughly studying all design-related issues, the next step is to decide which particular structure will meet your design protocols. Choosing the appropriate organizational structure can provide numerous benefits, such as reduced costs, greater growth potential, clearer decision-making authority and accountability, as well as better governance and policy clarification. Your structure also plays a key role in determining organizational behavior, culture, flexibility, and adaptiveness.

The organizational design process can lead to many different structural outcomes. Based on your strategic intent, these options include:

Hierarchical Line/Chain of Command—This bureaucratic, centralized, and pyramid-shaped structure embodies a more formal, vertical, and hierarchical structure with many lines of command. This structure is most popular and more suitable for complex and larger scale organizations with high degrees of standardization. A key benefit of vertical, hierarchical structures is faster decision-making, as these are usually made by the top person while involving fewer staff in doing so. Other benefits include clearer authority and responsibility lines, career paths. On the contrary, such a commanding style discourages creativity, innovation, and organizational adaptability. Amazon is an example of such a structure.

This hierarchical structure can also be divided by **Functional** design and activities with additional mid-level managers needed, which allows for greater specialization. Typically, there are formal organizational charts for each department; roles are clearly defined and accompanied by more rigid policies, SOPs, and constraints. Decisions can be slower, as each goes through the various levels of management. As this structure is more formal and controlled from the top, communication usually flows from top to bottom and the organization's ability of being adaptive to changing market conditions is hampered. Starbucks is structured by function.

Entrepreneurial—This pre-bureaucratic structural design is horizontal (flatter) and centrally controlled from the top, but with very little standardization of functions. The leader (or founder) makes most key decisions, and communication occurs through one-on-one dialogues. This is a predominate model for startups. Benefits include more open communication and speed. Yet, it can cause supervisory confusion and lead toward generalizing staff skill sets, and its structure is difficult to maintain during strong growth. Valve is an example of this structural type.

Divisional/Span of Control—This very common structure is set up around areas that include multi-functional activities and operations self-contained under one authority and group. Each group runs a separate profit and cost center. They can be organized by market segment (such as Walmart and Target), by product (as many technology firms), or by geographic area whereby each region or district may offer localized services and logistics, etc. These geographic locations may also have their own marketing, sales, and product teams. They usually rely on centralized corporate service groups (e.g., finance, legal, procurement, human resources) for shared services outside their span of control. McDonalds fits into this geographical structure type.

This structural type has numerous benefits: authority can be delegated, performance can be measured by each group, which brings greater ownership of results, and simpler processes result in more flexibility and specialization. However, such a structure can create unhealthy rivalries between divisions. Also, operational costs may increase due to duplication of resources. Lastly, staff may focus more on achieving their divisional goals compared to the organization's.

Divisional/Span of Control organizational types can structure their activities and decision-making by either centralizing them, decentralizing them, or a combination of both.

Centralization—Under a centralized structure, all activities, functions, operations, and decisions are managed from one central location, even if such operations are spread out globally, via separate, specialized departments. Yet, as they are self-contained, they can better integrate vertically to speed up production, if necessary. There is a high degree of standardization and formalization, which leads to operational efficiencies. This structure suits producers of specific, standardized products and services in larger volumes at lower costs. Communication is more rigid and occurs mainly within each department. This may lead to competing interests and in-fighting between groups, causing slowdowns, inflexibilities, and compromised cross-departmental cooperation.

Decentralization—A decentralized structure is the exact opposite, whereby operations are managed and decisions are made regionally or locally. Acting locally is seen as a benefit for speed, but conflicts may occur with the center office related to ultimate local resourcing and budget decisions (e.g., who foots the bill).

Centralization/Decentralization—Creating a combination of a centralized and decentralized structure may be warranted, but this approach takes delicate thought and care in deciding which activities and functions fit best under which department's management and decision-making. Going too far in either direction can confuse staff who try and work across both structures.

Matrix Structure—This post-bureaucratic structure involves the combining of resources from all business functions and regions to focus on a dedicated market segment. This hierarchical structure is vertical in design and resembles a grid. It presents a multi-dimensional perspective both internally and externally, by market segment, function, line of business, and geography. This structure may look good on paper, but it is difficult to seamlessly execute. However, it does allow to build teams that complement each other's strengths and weaknesses.

Accountability and authority should be directed to only one individual, which must be made very clear. For example, who (which individual) ultimately has the authority to act and decide what is to be done and when? This scenario usually plays out between two individuals: the functional manager and the project manager. Who has the ultimate responsibility or control? This must be communicated and made very clear to everyone involved.

Benefits of the matrix model include diminishing the vertical nature of all functions (the silo mentality), having more horizontal interactions between functions and activities, and being an enabler for specialization. On the negative side, power struggles between functional and project heads can occur, while chain of command issues create increased operational complexity. This may lead to staff confusion. Lastly, costs might increase as the ratio between management and staff also increases. Phillips is an example of this structural type.

Team Structure—This structure involved establishing formal teams by pulling together resources from other areas of functional expertise and organizing them by their competencies. The team leader should possess both accountability and authority to act in the team's best interests, as they are usually classified as a separate profit center. Such teams may work well, experience higher levels of productivity and agility, and require minimal management. However, each team member's "true" line supervisor still exists elsewhere. This creates a dual-reporting relationship of sorts. If each line supervisor is not supportive of the team's purpose or having their own direct subordinate seconded to it, they can create havoc on the team's efforts and overall performance. Career paths can also be less clear. Google is an example of such a structure.

Project Structure—This structure is similar and a subset to the team structure, but their time span of operating is shorter. They are usually responsible for their budget and own it. Project teams are established to deliver high-impact initiatives. Members are temporarily assigned to such projects until they are completed. To limit costs, the project members may remain remote and not all brought to one main location. Once the project is successfully completed, it is usually absorbed into the most logical operational unit of the organization. Some members may stay with the project, while others may go back to their original, pre-project roles.

All the structures discussed above are more traditional in nature. However, there are other more modern structural models that deserve mentioning.

Network/Virtual Structure—This structure is boundaryless and does not physically exist in a centralized location. Closely coupled networks of supplier alliance partners are established upstream while customer relationships are managed downstream. Most, if not all, activities are managed via the Internet. While the core of a typical virtual organization usually remains small, it operates on a low-cost basis. Virtual teams can also possess powerful global reach. In many instances, while selling and distributing smaller volumes of products and services, they can become market leaders within multiple niche segments. Benefits of this structure include greater flexibility, speed, empowerment, and decision-making. Cons include the difficultly in managing offsite processes and confusion in who has final authority. H&M (Hemes & Mauritz) is an example of this structural type.

Open-Value Network—These are transnational networks utilizing technologies to operate. There is no formal mechanism of power to control their platform or infrastructure that enable network activities. This model is held together by gamification tools as well as financial incentives linked to contributions and individual performance. An example of such an operation is Bitcoin.

> **Lessons Learned**
>
> Whichever organizational structure you choose, my advice is to carefully think through the corresponding decision architecture and decision-making rights and where the ultimate authority and accountability rests. If you get this aspect wrong, every structure's flaws will be magnified. revealed and magnified.

Lessons Learned

I have worked within each of the traditional structures described above, some with more success than others. I either inherited an existing structure upon arrival or created a new one based on our future strategic direction. I cannot state that there is one best organizational design. The key is to identify one that best aligns with and meets the needs of your strategic intent and team.

Many of my organizations utilized multiple mini-structures within our overall org. structure. But, again, the needs of your people talent should be your number one priority.

Leaders who have successfully operated within a traditional structure now require totally new skill sets and ways of thinking, behaving and acting to find success with the modern versions. The traditional and modern org. structures have become two distinct and different worlds.

What are your thoughts?

Does your organization's strategic intent lead to a distinct competitive advantage? Where and how might it be improved?

Is your strategic planning process efficient and effective? Does it involve all parts and the most relevant individuals within your organization? Who should be added to this process?

Do your strategies drive your financial planning or vice versa (e.g., which one is the primary focus)?

What is your preferred organizational structure and why?

What organizational structure do you currently work within and how might it be improved?

CHAPTER 6

Leadership and the Customer

Chapter Preview

- Why the Customer Experience (and an aligned service culture) has become a critical success factor, and how is it created

- The necessary components of a quality Customer Service program.

- "Key Performance Indicators" to measure, to better understand and improve your customer satisfaction levels.

- Why creating greater customer loyalty can lead to improved profits and sustainability

Without paying customers, you eventually have no business. It's that simple. Attracting, retaining, and expanding your customer base is a top priority. This is not as simple as it sounds. Effective leaders go to great lengths to ensure their organization understands, embraces, and is committed to delivering the ultimate customer experience. This encompasses offering quality end-to-end customer service while measuring and tracking satisfaction levels. The end game is building customer loyalty. This chapter delves into why the customer experience is so important and offers proven methods of how to achieve success.

> **Lessons Learned**
> Most organizations, including many of mine, believe they are achieving a higher level of customer service than their customers believe themselves to. Huge discrepancies exist and can only be identified and addressed through the implementation of some version of a CX model.

> **Lessons Learned**
> Delivering an inspiring CX resulting in high customer satisfaction and loyalty levels involves quality interactions before, during, and after the purchase. This requires a significant commitment, investment in resources, and funding for tools.

> **Lessons Learned**
> CX starts internally by putting your staff's satisfaction first, as this drives internal loyalty and productivity. Productivity drives value, which drives customer satisfaction. Customer satisfaction drives customer loyalty. Customer loyalty drives profitability and growth!

The Customer Experience

The customer experience, also referred to as CX, has become a top priority for most organizations. CX is about creating an aligned service culture to increase the quality of your service practices. This takes a holistic, top-to-bottom, end-to-end approach. CX is everyone's responsibility. It involves the continuous monitoring of how your customers respond to the pre-purchase (selling efforts), consumption (product usage), and post-sales (support) stages. If no follow up actions or improvements result from these customer interactions, inputs, and findings, you are probably wasting your time.

Are you consistently living up to the promises and commitments you have made to your customers? Whatever you and your team believe when answering this question is somewhat irrelevant, as this can only be answered from the perspective and perceptions of the customer.

To gather these CX insights, all customer interactions and experiences are to be tracked during each transaction with you, in a timely manner. Such information gathering may take the form of surveys as well as verbal interactions through customer and prospect forums. Customer Relationship Management (CRM) tools as well as social media platforms and applications are also efficient means to connect with customers through the creation of communities.

A customer having one bad experience at any time during their journey with you can result in lost business as each step is created equally. Bad customer experiences can occur due to differing and complex purchasing processes, negative customer support, long call waiting times, and ignorance of customer feedback. Thus, key goals of CX are to drive greater revenues, increase customer satisfaction and loyalty levels, while reducing churn rates (lost business).

To succeed here requires a total commitment across your organization, from the frontline to senior management. Success involves creating a corporate-wide CX vision with key statements as to how you will operate and behave. Detailed, executable plans need to be created as well as an appropriate and aligned structure through which to roll everything out. Identifying who your customers are as well as what they want and need is also a critical step.

This CX commitment should be reinforced by internal training and education as to how to create an emotional connection with customers. This is about "it's not what you say, but how you say it." Also, capturing real-time customer input, promptly acting on it, and developing tools to measure CX return on investment (ROI) is paramount.

Customer Service

In his latest of many books, "Uplifting Service," Ron Kaufman [19] masterfully spells out, among many other customer service (also referred to as CS) gems, his six levels of CS. While training is an important component in the mix (learning "what to do" in certain situations), Kaufman takes this notion a step further by making the point that our true purpose is to change "how to think" in such situations.

If I may paraphrase four of his six levels of CS, they are:

Expected—Whereby the basic CS terms are fulfilled, but at an average level of service.

Desired—This level is above basic as you are aware of the way the customer wants the relationship to work.

Surprising—Providing an unexpected level of service the customer likes by offering distinctive value.

Unbelievable—This is an astonishing level of service that usually happens just once. If you repeat the same level of service, chances are you will go back to a lower level as the customer's expectations of you are now automatically higher. Unless you do even better, "unbelievable" will not be the result.

There are also two levels of service lower than "Expected":

Below—Providing a customer with the bare minimum, but the service might be late, not of the highest quality and/or your CS interactions may not have been professional.

Criminal—While not strictly illegal, of course, a terrible customer experience is provided as you broke your promises.

Lessons Learned

There are many takeaways here, but my main one is that CS is a moving target and (as per Kaufman) much like an escalator going downward. If your CS service levels stand still, not improving, you will automatically continue to go downward as well. Thus, to improve your service levels, you need to continuously "step up!"

I highly suggest you invite Ron Kaufman to lead an onsite workshop as we did. It is certainly "uplifting!"

What is the best way to organize and structure your CS efforts in a global environment? My experience brings me to the following recommendations for consideration if you conduct business internationally:

From a logistical standpoint, establish your customer call centers in your major "hub" time zones and regions that you serve. This allows you to act locally and in the multiple languages necessary. This location "spread" gives your customers 24/7 access to you if you use appropriate tools. On the other hand, having one or two centralized call centers serving the world can be disastrous for timely and efficient support, not to mention having staff working crazy and unhealthy shifts. I have witnessed both scenarios and support local access.

Locating your call centers is the first step. Next comes the harder challenge, staffing them with a qualified team of personable and polite professionals. Additional skill sets I seek to instill in training focus mostly on soft skills, including empathy, adaptability, communication (i.e., listening, problem-solving, and conflict management), interpersonal skills, sales acumen, a sense of speed, and attention to detail (accuracy).

Dealing with customer complaints occurs quite frequently and is a main activity for CS. If staff are trained with a short-term view, a problem may be addressed, but it will continue to reoccur. Addressing this dilemma requires management to track the areas where the number of complaints are the highest and of a similar nature.

The focus should be on issue identification and conducting a root cause analysis of them. Some of the issues may be interdependent, so addressing one may assist in dealing with others simultaneously. Doing this successfully should reduce related complaint call volumes tremendously.

CS competencies that can positively influence and improve your service levels based on customer input are dependability, responsiveness, authority to act, empathy, and quality assurance. These and more should be part of your regular CS indoctrination program.

Next, you should establish varying levels of support expertise for your CS team members:

- A basic first level of support for all incoming calls whereby simple inquiries (e.g., invoice errors, contact detail updates) can be promptly addressed.

- A middle level of support that can deal with issues that require a minimal level of understanding of the nature of the product or service (e.g., sending new data files, revised data dumps).

- A top-tier level of service offering professional advice by SMEs (subject matter experts).

A commitment to an integrated technology system and tools will allow for seamless internal team interactions and efficient handoffs to higher levels during all customer touchpoints and should improve their overall service experience.

Automated voice technologies (AVT) and artificial intelligence (AI), while very prevalent, have their limitations, particularly in comprehending complex customer problems. If asked, most customers (including me) still prefer

Lessons Learned

Over the years, consumer behavioralists have shared that most consumers buy based on emotions, then justify their purchase later with logic. As a buyer myself, I fully support this premise. This field of study is focused on the buyer behaviors of individuals and groups. Influencers of buyer behavior include the buyer's lifestyle, economic status, occupation, age, personality, and self-esteem.

to interact with a "live" person. Few like to deal with a voice recording or be put on hold or into an endless loop of multi-layered, sequential numerical options to choose from. I usually just hang up and go elsewhere, if possible.

Finally, ensure your CS teams are happy and engaged. This leads to them offering better service, resulting in happier customers. Otherwise, low CS staff satisfaction and poor engagement efforts by management are directly linked to lesser customer satisfaction levels. Your internal CS staff (as well as all others) are your customers too.

The stages each buyer goes through to make a purchase are similar. It starts with a recognition or awareness of an unsatisfied need, called a stimulus. Then, the buyer undertakes a search and evaluation of alternative product choices. Lastly, a purchase is made followed by some form of post-purchase behavior. Such a purchase process is heavily determined by consumer perceptions based on their closest associates, affiliates, or friends and family.

Customer Satisfaction

Customer satisfaction, also known as CSAT, is a foundational component of the CX process. It is one of the most important marketing metrics as a high level of CSAT leads to greater customer retention and loyalty, which leads to greater profits.

CSAT is based on each customer's perception and their judgement of personal fulfillment (either high or low). It is derived from the difference between a product's expected value to a customer and the actual value delivered to them. In other words, it is a metric of the difference between the value proposition that an organization promised the customer and the value that the customer receives. As suggested by marketing guru Philip Kotler, [20] satisfaction is a measurement of personal feelings of pleasure or disappointment resulting from an organization's perceived performance and outcome vs. the customer's own expectations.

CSAT levels can easily shift based on each customer interaction. Knowing how happy or unhappy your customers are will alert you to what is working and where service gaps exist, needing your prompt attention. Your total customer base is broader than just the users of your products and services and includes your employees, vendors, suppliers, and partners. These should be tracked, as each may be in contact with your direct customers.

Those organizations that actively track CSAT metrics want to have their customers to be categorized as "highly satisfied." This outcome is very difficult to achieve. When a new customer starts out as highly satisfied, the bar for their future expectations has now been set very high. Over time and based on their preliminary high level of satisfaction, as they receive the same level of service again, they drop back to the category of being "just satisfied." As a high level of service is regularly repeated, the customer soon perceives it as becoming average or below. Ron Kaufman refers to this outcome as the "downward escalator effect." [19]

When reviewing the large databases of a typical organization's CSAT levels, holistically, the bell curve tends to also skew to the middle of mediocrity. This skewing limitation effect is reinforced by the fact that most dissatisfied customers usually go elsewhere. Thus, their lower satisfaction scores cease to be tracked and skew the lower end scores upward.

There are other limitations to tracking CSAT scores. A CSAT score does not necessarily measure overall value or quality. As CSAT scores are based on a customer's perception at a given point in time, their mood swings when completing a survey may change day to day, becoming a moving target.

Is the goal of achieving 100 percent total customer satisfaction realistic? Conceptually, this sounds good. But it can cost you by negatively affecting your profits. For example, you may overdeliver to certain customers in the hope of increasing their perceived value. This new service level may come with its own cost increase to better serve them, yet not always with a corresponding price increase. The math here is simple. You have increased your cost of service but kept your price the same, thus your profit is lower (e.g., revenue minus cost equals profit).

Nevertheless, CSAT measurements are not going away anytime soon, but additional customer tracking metrics can give you a broader picture in relation to your CSAT scores. These include tracking customer loyalty, their referral likelihood, and profit per customer, to name a few.

If you decide to use CSAT metrics, this requires employing strong, consistent, and credible local account management staff and having consistent practices in place. If financially feasible, frontline account management efforts are best suited to gathering customer issues firsthand as well as supporting a more appreciated "human touch." Such continuous customer input needs to be captured into some form of CRM (Customer Relationship Management) system and followed up on. This process is also referred to as capturing the "voice of the customer," or VOC. [21]

Try to avoid the "black hole syndrome." This trap refers

Lessons Learned

While useful, market research and surveys are not always the best tools available to monitor satisfaction levels as to what is on your customer's mind. Usually, the participants' responses are based on their moods at that point in time. And their moods are constantly shifting. I have found that market research rarely gives you an "aha" moment whereby you learn something major that you did not already know or expect. My experience has shown me that most research only reinforces what you already know, just providing comfort. If you truly want to gather more useful market insights, try to discover what your nonusers are thinking about and why they are not purchasing from you.

to not closing out your customers' outstanding issues or complaints. Neglecting such input will quickly lead to it ceasing to be received and passed along as the customer and your local account management team will likely stop sharing such input. This "lose-lose" situation occurs more than we think.

CSAT levels and customer retention are directly linked. If you are skeptical of this statement, perhaps the following statistics will convince you. [22] Only 12 to 14 percent of customers defect for product reasons, yet 8 percent defect due to poor post-sale service treatment. They are four times more likely to switch brands if their customer service experience is negative. The cost to attract a new customer is five to twenty-five times higher than saving a customer from defecting.

On a more positive note, 89 percent of customers are more likely to repurchase after a positive customer service experience and three out of five report quality customer service is a key to building their loyalty.

Remember, customer needs never go away, but what changes is how you satisfy them. Activities focused on new customer acquisition as well as optimizing the value of existing customers to retain them should lead to an increase in profits. Be creative!

Customer Loyalty

This is achieved when customers go to the effort of establishing a longer association and affiliation with your brand, products, and/or services. Loyal customers usually patronize your organization more often. Their satisfaction and trust levels are higher than most of your other customers. Once again, the statistics speak for themselves related to the value of customer loyalty. [23–24] Within the US, 77 percent of customers have stayed loyal to specific brands for more than ten years. On average, these loyal customers spend 67 percent more than new customers.

A critical element that is driving these behaviors is loyalty programs. 90 percent of consumers state they would choose a brand that offers such enticing programs over a lower priced competitor who does not. 72 percent are even more loyal with their purchasing power when they are offered personalized "premium" programs. The top premium perks they prefer are free shipping (66 percent), instant discounts (60 percent), surprise rewards (45 percent), and exclusive offers (35 percent). With an average of 80 percent of a business's profits coming from their top 20 percent of its customer base, it is tremendously important for the leader to continue to make creative efforts to retain as well as expand their loyalty base.

It is obvious that customer retention is very important. So, what are some strategies to implement to improve customer loyalty and achieve financial success?

- Plan to provide excellent customer service from the start. Listen to and respond to your customers. Regularly ask your loyal customers for input on newly proposed products and services, redesigned packaging, etc. This effort should drive greater customer appreciation and engagement.

- Reward loyal customers. Create personalized, digitized premium programs for your most loyal customers to make them feel more important.

- Enhance the customer experience by using the data collected to better understand your customers' buying behaviors, purchase patterns, demographics, etc. With their permission, you can proactively send special offers related to the products and services they most frequently purchase or details on other related and complementary products and services that may appeal to them.

> **Lessons Learned**
>
> Loyalty plays a key role in our personal relationships with family, friends, and other loved ones. It brings a higher level of commitment and dedication between people. Knowing you can count on each other when problems arise and have someone to turn to can be comforting. Yet, building such personal loyalty is not easy. It requires a significant mutual effort of time, feelings, and letting your guard down.

> **Lessons Learned**
>
> A useful survey tool to measure customer loyalty is the Net Promoter Score (NPS) developed by consulting firm, Bain and Co. Asking customers three to four specific questions can tell you the likelihood of a customer referring your service to others. Referrals are very important related to influencing buyer behaviors and creating loyalty, an indication of future growth.[26]

- While acting with a human touch is critical, many customers have simple inquires that can be addressed by posting a set of frequently asked questions (FAQs) on your website. Gaining prompt answers to FAQs saves time and money on both sides.

Customer purchase decisions are influenced by personal experiences, brand reputation, as well as recommendations from friends, family, and trusted peers. Loyal customers "voluntarily" choose your brand and services. The "best" products and services do not always win in every situation. If you focus on and succeed in accomplishing the three Rs of loyalty (customer retention, related cross and upselling opportunities, and customer referrals), you are on the right track. Paulo Claussen, a marketing executive, offers a different spin on the three "Rs." His include rewards (how to gain and receive them), relevance (to deepen the customers engagement), and recognition (better offers to gain longer term loyalty). [25]

In summary, loyal customers bring your organization many benefits, such as repeat business, more spending per transaction, and more referrals. They are a good defense mechanism against competition and are more forgiving when you make a mistake that negatively affects them.

> **Lessons Learned**
>
> When I was a Sales Manager, I would always ask my new and somewhat naïve sales recruits the same question related to doing business with a new customer. "Would they prefer to have the best product or the best customer relationships?" Every one of them said "the best product." I would then challenge them as my experience showed that strong relationships are better and more valuable. Here's my rationale: A customer who purchases but does not know you at all, but believes your product or service is the best, will quickly defect from you, if they are experiencing a problem, or when a better service comes along. Chances are, you will never know of this defection until after the fact, as they have no personal or emotional ties with you whatsoever. Thus, no contact from them to you will occur beforehand. However, if such strong personal ties exist, they will usually reach out to you before such a defection, allowing you the opportunity to fix the issue or offer another alternative solution. Many times, my customers would tell me that my service offering was not the best on the market, but they bought from me anyway. Trust me on this one, strong relationships and loyalty win out in most instances.

What are your thoughts?

Are potential impacts on your customer base taken into consideration in relation to every action or decision made?

Would your organization benefit from creating a corporate wide CX plan? How can you assist in making this a reality?

How do you rate your CS levels (e.g., where are you performing well and not)? Where can improvements be achieved?

What CSAT metrics does your organization measure? What new KPIs (key performance indicators) and customer insights can benefit your service levels?

Does your organization offer a loyalty program? What specific premium and personalized programs can be added to drive greater customer loyalty?

CHAPTER 7

Leadership and Innovation: Process and Product

Chapter Preview

- The five levels of "discovery skills" that successful CEOs utilize to drive innovation.

- A list of corporation innovation "killers" that exist in many organizations.

- Where to look and questions to ask to identify new innovations.

- The leader's role in fostering greater innovation.

Steve Jobs once said, "Innovation distinguishes between a leader and a follower." [27] Who do you want to be?

Innovation comes in many shapes and sizes from a new product, a new and improved way of doing something, process or workflow improvements, or new ways of thinking. There are also technical innovations coming from such activities as research and development (R&D) as well as redesign efforts that impact production and consumption efficiencies and effectiveness. "Simplification" is also a smart avenue for innovation.

Innovation impacts both process and product. It is about applied creativity, practical implementation, and pragmatic transformation of new ideas. Such creative insights are cognitive but require emotional competencies to persuade and influence others.

There are four basic stages to a creative act:

- Take adequate time to immerse yourself and others into the identified problem or opportunity to be addressed.
- Gather relevant data and informational details to review, incubate, and brainstorm.
- Clarify to better understand once breakthrough or promising ideas are identified.
- Execute on one (or more) of the ideas through prompt action.

Academic researchers and authors Dyer, Gregerson, and Christensen developed a comprehensive and effective methodology for approaching innovation based on quality input from the world's top CEO innovators. Their findings are categorized and focused on five levels of "discovery skills" that these CEOs exhibited to better innovate. [28]

L1: Associating—Having the ability to connect disparate thoughts, ideas, and concepts that few others imagined feasible.

L2: Questioning—Asking provocative questions that challenge conventional wisdom or the status quo. As Peter Drucker stated, "It's more about asking the right question vs. finding the right answer."

L3: Observing—Directly observing someone doing their job and experientially following the tasks they perform and are trying to complete.

L4: Experimenting—It is prudent to conduct constructive experiments to test and validate new ideas.

L5: Networking—Make efforts to meet with others who think and act differently from you. Attending conferences, events, and forums are a viable means of doing this. Also, I recommend assigning a few of your team members to take on work assignments elsewhere in the world to gain insights from other work cultures.

Lessons Learned

Try your best to not quickly shoot down or kill another's ideas. Brainstorming is more about idea generation, not providing immediate answers or solutions.

Lessons Learned

We used the direct observation technique when developing a new app from an existing service that our customers (airlines, airports and travel agents) would use to pre-validate passports and visas to check in passengers onto flights. By observing customers being checked in, we discovered our tool was very slow, cumbersome, clumsy, and not comprehensive enough to adequately address numerous outstanding issues in a timely manner. Based on our findings, we re-engineered the app to remove all these flaws and more. The new app allows the user to automatically determine whether or not a passenger's passport and visa are valid for the flight they are planning to take. This service has become the market leader.

Lessons Learned

I like to refer to innovation as the "wow," factor as this is the response most people give when they witness innovative breakthroughs. I routinely ask my colleagues to search for wow factors by putting themselves in the prospective user's shoes and asking what's in it for them?

Lessons Learned

I rarely launch a new product or service without having it market-tested or piloted by potential users. This process allows us to spend our investment dollars more wisely, while ensuring a greater likelihood of market success. With an average failure rate for new products and services of over 50 percent, you can avoid losing a lot of time, money, and your reputation through comprehensive market testing.

Even with these great methods to generate ideas and drive innovation within your organization, there are organizational "innovation killers" that can hamper future successes. These include, but are not limited to:

- Short-sightedness, as in judging innovation projects by the same financial parameters as existing products (e.g., using the same ROI, profit margin, payback period).
- Micromanaging, as in the team or an individual receiving constant scrutiny from above.
- Overcontrol, as in holding critical "go/no go" reviews too early in the incubation process.
- Under-control, as in holding critical "go/no go" reviews too late in the process.
- Overoptimism, as in giving too aggressive timelines to achieve success.

As a product manager, I have unfortunately and painfully lived through all of these. As a leader, I vowed not to repeat them.

How many times have you heard a leader state, "We need more good ideas?" I have heard this comment ad nauseam. Such a trite comment causes tremendous frustration among the ranks, as it is neither factual nor helpful.

Often, underperformance is less a problem of lacking good ideas but more so about what is done with the ideas being submitted for review. Most ideas never have a chance of moving forward due to corporate risk aversion and uncertainty on the part of upper management. Or their development is stopped prematurely due to early setbacks.

If upper management is willing to accept some failures as part of the product developmental process, some new product outcomes may end more positively. [29] For example, WD-40 became a success after thirty-nine failed attempts. James Tyson tested 5271 vacuum prototypes without securing a license agreement. Thus, he built his own manufacturing facility. Steve Jobs started Apple in 1976, was ousted in 1985, came back in 1997 (under a new board). The rest is history. Without persistence and a sharp, new leader, some of these successful products might never have occurred, which would have been a shame.

From a process perspective, many unique innovations come by way of cross-functional, integrated initiatives. The best and most relevant ideas for new product development (NPD) usually come from those closest to the market and customers, not from the top of the organization.

Innovation can also occur by not always adding complexities but rather by eliminating them (simplification). Other related areas of innovation and transformation to investigate may include pursuing alternate business models as to how you operate and serve customers more efficiently and effectively. Rethinking the sourcing of your supply chains or relocating manufacturing or production may also have merit.

Other intriguing questions to ask yourself include:

- Can more processes be automated to replace manual processes? Unfortunately, this path may lead to people being eliminated where little to no value is being added based on their current tasks. Autonomous vehicles, drones, contactless deliveries, smart robots with artificial intelligence (AI) are breakthrough examples of such innovations.

- What role are blockchain and crowdsourcing playing in decentralizing finance as an interesting and more efficient alternative means to raising new capital?

- How do creative virtual interfaces (e.g., virtual reality used for training purposes) and other digital interactions provide alternatives to visiting a "bricks and mortar" building? Such technologies can also allow for a "try before you buy" model.

These should spark your appetite to continue questioning where other possible innovations might exist.

Lessons Learned

Upon joining a new organization, I learned that their track record for developing new products was dismal. Products were developed, but never launched, or, if they were, they often missed the market window by being late with a savvier competitor storming in ahead of us.

When we mapped out our existing NPD process, we discovered that we had 126 distinct input and signoff steps in place for each new product, no matter how big or small the investment. I promptly set up a small cross-functional team of my most savvy, rational and smart colleagues to fix this. They set up a "war room" and visually represented these 126 steps on the four surrounding walls. In a matter of a few months, they reengineered this process down to just fifteen steps! We communicated these new NPD guidelines internally, which truly liberated our organization. Future NPD revenues grew significantly as a result.

Lessons Learned

When one of my organizations was experiencing a challenging financial year, I set up an organization-wide contest. Whoever came up with the biggest cost-saving idea (that was actually implemented and the savings achieved) would earn a 10 percent commission on the total savings. No investments to implement the ideas were allowed. The one other caveat was the ideas could not originate within their own department or job function because I expect creative ideas from them as part of their responsibilities.

Needless to say, the excitement and ideas were flying around the building. The winner walked away with a $10,000 check and we netted $90,000 to our bottom line. Other cost-saving ideas of lesser amounts were also implemented, but no rewards were paid.

Lessons Learned

One of my organizations was hindered by a tremendously slow new contract approval and signature process. It took us months to send executed copies back to customers. This was customer service at its worst and an embarrassing way to begin a new working relationship.

With a great team effort, we were able to gain internal finance, legal, and line-of-business approval to allow each manager to sign off simultaneously (vs. consecutively). We reduced the current bottleneck tremendously. We also gained true visibility as to how long some contracts sat on certain individuals' desks before approval. It was the same culprits every time. Peer pressure changed their behaviors.

We also gained internal support to begin legally accepting digital customer contract signatures as fully executed. In the past, hard copies were our only acceptable means. Sometimes, paper contracts being sent internationally via parcel post "snail mail" could take weeks, if not longer. Needless to say, our new customers and internal staff were both very pleased with the change to digital contracts.

Product innovation comes in two forms:

- **Sustaining**—Incremental and easy-to-implement product improvements
- **Disruptive**—Enhancements requiring users to change how they utilize the new offering

Disruptive market innovations may displace established products or even make them obsolete based on new usage preferences and/or functionalities. Along the same lines, new and innovative processes allow combinations of unique outputs and deliveries that did not exist before. Clayton Christensen has authored intriguing research articles and books on this topic. [30]

Rapid innovations in both process and product have long been a focal point for leaders. Now, it is less about the speed of the innovations themselves but more about how and where these new market disruptors will occur. One example of this phenomenon is the advent of "Big Data." This opportunity is less about the magnitude and volume of new disparate data sets that are now available at an organization's fingertips and more about the new tools that allow it to be combined in logical formats for valuable predictive analytics and better decision-making.

Leaders no longer rely on their traditional "gut" decisions, as there is a "new normal." Cloud infrastructures are allowing for real-time global access to Big Data anytime and anywhere. According to Gartner [31], global IT (information technology) spending is forecast to reach $4.4 trillion in 2022 (a 5.3% increase over 2021). While global access to such relevant and timely technology resources is a positive step in the right direction, this reopens the door to data privacy, security, and intellectual property (IP) issues needing to be satisfactorily addressed.

Related to this chapter title, "Leadership and Innovation," a significant decision should also be reached as to where innovation "sits" within your organization. Is it a separate, stand-alone team (think tank) or to be embedded within each product department? I support the latter, but with a twist: each business unit owns their decentralized innovation process supported by a centralized team for conducting research, reporting, building prototypes, and negotiating vendor agreements. This approach eliminates redundant or repetitive activities.

A more important question remains: What is the leader's role in innovation? Is their responsibility to guide and facilitate the innovation process or to actively add and test their own ideas? I support the latter approach, but a solid and "in-tune" leader can play both roles. Based on recent research, many of the top leaders of the most successful companies today say they spend at least 50 percent of their time on innovation discovery activities. [28] Are you one of them?

Lessons Learned

Innovation requires a shift in corporate culture, values, and behaviors to encourage nontraditional thinking and support experimentation. A new philosophy needs to be established, capabilities need to be built through training, resources need to be allocated, rewards need to be aligned, and a tolerance for taking calculated risks needs to be developed. Mistakes need not be punished unless they are continuously repeated.

Lessons Learned

It is short-sighted to judge innovation projects by the same financial parameters as existing products. Using the same ROI (return on investment), profit margin, payback period, etc. is wishful thinking. In doing so, you run the risk of killing them for missing unrealistic, preset financial criteria. These new ideas need more patience and a longer horizon to be judged and evaluated.

Lessons Learned

We were a leading higher education publisher in the business discipline of accounting. Our Introductory Principles publications were mature, perceived as out of date and losing their relevance. We had to act and act fast.

By staying in close contact with those trying to revive and modernize the Introductory Accounting curriculum and listening closely to the concerns and complaints of corporate clients who were hiring unprepared accounting graduates, we devised a plan to address a market need with an innovative solution.

We produced the first, revolutionary Introductory Accounting publication with no debits or credits (e.g., no bookkeeping). Instead of walking the reader through the traditional format of how accounting transactions affect the balance sheet, our author creatively took a real-world and pragmatic business activities approach. The reader now learned how, where, and why accounting is used to assist in business decisions while applying critical thinking skills. This approach was not without its market acceptance risks.

It was a big hit and, as it had no competition, it became an overnight sensation in both accounting and business school curriculums. Unit sales went through the roof. It was a pleasure to see our competitors scrambling to develop their own versions. While we had a two-year head start on them, we did not "sit on our laurels." By the time they responded to our first edition, we simultaneously launched our second edition, outsmarting the competition and setting them back once again. Big risk, big rewards!

Lessons Learned

Setting up an innovation "seed fund" is a great, low-risk way to assess, test, and pilot NPD ideas. With as little as $25–100K, you can easily determine if a new product concept warrants additional funding. I created and led such an incubator fund with great results (e.g., a success rate on such investments of +68 percent). Predetermined financial metrics and nonfinancial outcomes were agreed upon to gain funding. My approval process for securing funds was completed within twenty-four to forty-eight hours. Many of these NPD ideas went on to take dominant market positions and were highly profitable.

What are your thoughts?

Is innovation a key part of your organizational culture related to strategic and operational planning? How might such behaviors and execution be improved?

Is calculated risk-taking encouraged by senior management and mistakes considered a learning experience?

Can you identify two to three areas where process improvements can drive greater productivity, reduce costs, and increase profits?

What factors have led to your organization's best P&S (Product and Service) successes as well as failures (and what are the lessons learned from both)?

Part 2

Management

CHAPTER 8

Effective Management Defined

Chapter Preview

- Key principles and functions where effective managers excel.
- Key practices and actions that effective managers utilize.
- How do effective managers address underperformance
- The most important skill sets effective managers possess.
- Examples of crucial business activities and their link to the four management functions (Planning, Organizing, Directing, and Control).

An organization's success is based on many factors, including the effectiveness of its management. Effective managers are fair, yet demanding, and operate with a sense of urgency. They are reliable, persistent, and they take calculated business risks, while remaining forgiving when mistakes are made. This is necessary to drive innovation.

Management Principles

Management is about acting in the present. However, effective managers must continue to reinforce and remind their teams not to lose focus on the big picture (their Vision). Everything they do today should be a stepping-stone for tomorrow. Continuously reinforcing this short-term Mission, and long-term Vision connection is paramount. Many managers unfortunately focus first on the "what," then make their way to "how," and finally the "why." This order should be reversed. [3] Effective managers bring order, consistency, and productivity by aligning employees on a common platform while getting the most out of them. Effective managers challenge conventional wisdom and shake things up. They dig below the surface to identify barriers and obstacles and address them by actively involving their staff in problem-solving and the change process. Active listening and continuous learning on the manager's part are critical to this process. Asking questions and conducting an open and honest dialogue allows a manager's staff to feel comfortable in sharing more accurate and critically important information.

Managers focus on putting first things first through prioritization to accomplish certain tasks, activities, and initiatives. This is accomplished by creating a mission statement (see Chapter 4) and then aligning your staff around it. While people and mission go hand in hand, as Colin Powell put it, "You can count more on people than your plans." People are your most important asset, and they deserve your utmost time and attention. [32]

Successful management is all about:

- Executing your business strategies through organizational administration.

- Adhering to rules and policies with impartiality.

- Coordinating with staff.

- Creating a quality work environment.

- Keeping staff satisfaction levels high.

- Aligning skill sets to functional activities, systems architecture, and process alignment.

- Allocating financial resources.

Effective managers do not micromanage but have detailed knowledge of the business. If you cannot master the details, you cannot master the big picture. [32] Missing small details can end up becoming detrimental to executing your mission.

In his book about Abraham Lincoln's leadership and management abilities, Donald Phillips shared many of Lincoln's management practices that made him so successful. [33] A few of these I utilize are:

- Walk around and be visible to your team. Get to know them in their own workspace. Many of your colleagues can become intimidated while in your office. Show a pleasant demeanor and ask a lot of questions to get to know them better.

- Create a community and build strong alliances with a few individuals whom you can confide in and who are authentic.

- Be decisive, persistent, persuasive.

- Keep your composure and sense of humor.

- Keep a positive outlook on things by being enthusiastic.

- Exude confidence and hopefulness.

- Utilize the art of storytelling.

- Do not just talk, take action, and avoid inaction.

What is the difference between an effective manager and a mediocre manager? Colin Powell sums it up quite well. [32] Mediocre managers carry out tasks and orders and then wait passively for more, while effective managers proactively take action.

Effective managers assume "If I have not explicitly been told no, I can do it" compared to mediocre managers who think "If I have not explicitly been told yes, I cannot do it." Mediocre managers tend to watch the clock, while effective managers focus on results. Effective managers feel responsible and "own" the results. They put forth their best efforts, as they understand that if they do not, others will not either.

There has been much study completed in the field of "what great managers do" as well as the common managerial skills that strong managers possess. One body of work was completed by Marcus Beckingham and the HBR (*Harvard Business Review*) through extensive research and by surveying approximately 80,000 managers. [34] According to Beckingham, great managers identify what is unique about each colleague and then capitalize on this individuality. They value these unique abilities and coordinate and integrate them into a plan instead of trying to change them. They turn individual talents and idiosyncrasies into strong performance by gleaning the most out of people. Instead of changing or transforming the individual, they tweak their role to capitalize on such uniqueness and their natural abilities. Then they match individual strengths and weaknesses, creating high-performance teams based on these interdependencies.

Buckingham uses an analogy of great managers: "they play chess and not checkers." In checkers, there is uniformity, as all pieces move the same way and are interchangeable. However, in chess, there is distinctiveness to each piece, as each of them moves in a different way. Great managers identify and effectively deploy skill set differences. These managers then work to "trigger" such strengths through non-financial reward and recognition programs. Such programs have been proven to be a more important incentive than receiving money. A key factor here is to match these trigger rewards to what the recipient values the most when being recognized. It could be time with the manager and/or their team members, access to select subject matter experts and/or a larger set of peers, or the ability to share their success story with the whole organization.

How does an effective manager address and overcome the underperformance of individuals on their team? There are three main learning styles (based on learning theory) that managers can apply based on an individual's preference to learning. [35] These styles can be offered on their own or in some combination:

- **Analyzing**—Some individuals learn best by analyzing a situation by taking each task apart, examining the elements, gathering the details, and then reconstructing them. The most powerful moments of this learning style come before the actual performance. This method works well in a classroom setting.

- **Doing**—Some individuals learn best by doing the task themselves and the most powerful moments of this style come during performance, through trial and error. An example is on-the-job training.

- **Watching**—Some individuals learn best by watching others do a task. They observe the total performance and witness how it all comes together. The most powerful moments of this learning style come after the performance.

Effective managers can offer individual training to underperformers or link them with a complimentary colleague whose strengths balance against the other's weaknesses. Another method is to apply more discipline and structured processes to the learner's job tasks. Lastly, the manager may have to rearrange the work of the underperformer to avoid the individual's weaknesses. My suggestion is to utilize these tactics in the order they are presented based on when progress is reached.

What are the most important skills that effective managers must possess? A research survey conducted by James Manktelow and Julian Birkinshaw asked this important question to approximately 15,000 managers. [36] The responses were quite extensive and are hard to argue against. I will focus on those I believe are the most critically important managerial competencies that I have utilized with the most success. I have chosen to categorize and combine some of these, as they overlap. They include:

- **Communication**—Possessing good communication skills allows you to share clear goals, objectives, and expectations as well as give recognition where it is due. Such interpersonal skills are critical for interacting with others and building strong relationships. Communication also involves active listening. This ability allows you to gather and retain important details and efficiently pass them along to others.

- **Emotional Intelligence**—Being adaptable and resilient while showing empathy and building mutual trust are key skills all managers should perfect. This starts with your ability to understand yourself and then others. Being competent at these "soft skills" will ensure your personal and professional lives are more productive and enjoyable. Empowering, delegating, engaging, and being able to read your team's emotions and responding appropriately will enlighten them as well. These social skills are a must when developing your best people talent.

- **Prioritization**—Your ability to put first things first, while understanding your end game, will take you a long way toward achieving organizational objectives and targets. Identifying and organizing the most critical success factors, roles, tasks, actions, processes, and appropriate structure will allow for the efficient use of your valuable time. In this way, you should be able to accomplish more in less time. Upfront planning allows you to properly organize activities, set guidelines and steps as to the wisest path to undertake, and execute your plan.

- **Problem-solving**—Anticipating, tackling, overcoming, and eliminating obstacles require your strong persistence, diligence, and perseverance.

- **Decision-making**—Being decisive allows you to act fast. Combining this with critical thinking allows you to objectively analyze various options and view issues from different perspectives with a focus on thinking first, then taking appropriate action. Thinking beyond today and into the future brings an added strategic dimension into play.

- **Teamwork**—Working as a collective team and promoting cohesion provides greater results than any individual can achieve alone. Collaboration should occur both within and outside of your team. Recruit a diverse team with complimentary skill sets. Successfully resolving disagreements and conflicts, eliminating obstacles, and establishing harmony are also important related skills.

A universal and crucial management practice utilized regularly by top managers to implement innovative, proven, tried, tested, and successful ideas is the use of an industry's "best practices." These provide an alternate avenue when appropriate know-how, competencies, and skills are not internally apparent or available to you.

Derived in 1905 and documented as "the best method and procedure, etc.," the modern term best practices was first recorded between 1980–1985. Best practices are procedures, guidelines, methods, or techniques that are widely accepted as superior or the most effective way to work based on a quality standard. Some industry and government bodies also adopt these and may mandate organizations within each industry do the same.

Best practices can be measured by assessments or audits, which bring numerous benefits such as saving time and money while improving results. Successfully implementing best practices can elevate your brand in the minds of customers. Their use may also eliminate certain problems or reoccurring mistakes currently faced within your organization.

> **Lessons Learned**
>
> Conducting research is a simple way to discover best practices that may be of benefit to your organization. Such research efforts should go beyond the scope of your own industry. Best practices tend to evolve over time as newer processes continue to be developed. Thus, continuous efforts to stay abreast of the latest quality processes is paramount.

> **Lessons Learned**
>
> Effective managers need the skills to change processes that may have been written in stone for many years. Staff tend to become very comfortable and complacent with how they work and may resist such change even if the change may bring them possible benefits.
>
> Managing in times of "crisis" is also a skill that managers should plan for and perfect. To be effective, I have found the need for change must be recognized and agreed upon, the status quo must be challenged, barriers must be removed, and your change agents (champions) must be internally recruited and play a leading role in supporting you.

Per Peter Drucker's "Theory of Management and Management Principles," effective managing and leading encompasses a broad range of activities that fall under four main operational functions or categories. [37] Effective managers should be strong and able to successfully implement and execute all of these.

Planning

Understanding where your organization is now, where you want to go, and how you will get there underpins the planning process. This allows for a predetermined course of action to be deployed, including defining your strategy, goal setting, and coordinating subplans. How you plan to reach decisions on these processes is also very important. Once these decisions are made, they must be bound by clear performance objectives and target alignment. An operating budget should be established to provide the necessary funds to execute your plans.

Abraham Lincoln summed up the importance of planning when he stated, "If I were given six hours to cut down a tree, I would spend the first four hours sharpening my axe." [33]

Some examples of planning activities include:

- Establishing your Vision and Mission statements (see Chapter 4).

- Creating your Strategic Intent and Business Plans (see Chapter 5).

- Staff Succession Planning (see Chapter 4).

- The Performance Management process (see Chapter 10).

- Creating a CX plan and quality customer service culture (see Chapter 6).

Organizing

This function involves establishing the appropriate organizational structure, design, and decision-making process to appropriately deliver your plans. This includes determining what tasks need to be completed and by whom. A workforce and materials plan as well as division of activities should be laid out as well. Integrating all activities and delegating the work effort in a cooperative environment will be beneficial. This process involves taking a holistic view of such activities from all angles (i.e., vertical, horizontal, internal, and external).

Some historical as well as modern management experts include "staffing" as a separate management function. While not undermining its importance, I agree with those who include it under "Organizing." Having the right people talent is crucial.

The staffing process includes conducting an inventory of your staff's skill sets and then putting the right people in the right jobs. Staff selection, renumeration, training, and development are also tasks to be undertaken here. When necessary, recruiting externally allows you to expand your staff knowledge base and experience levels, and should bring in new and fresh ways of thinking. The art of mastering quality interviewing techniques cannot be overemphasized, as poor recruiting results are very costly in many ways.

Some examples of organizing activities include:

- Organizational Design and Structure (see Chapter 5).
- Staffing and creating high-performance teams (see Chapter 11).
- Addressing staff skill set and cultural diversity inclusion (see Chapter 4).

Directing

The Planning and Organizing functions prepare the work to be done, while Directing is the actual execution of your plan. This process involves guiding, motivating, influencing, and leading your staff. Decisive decision-making, establishing delegation by authority level, and creating a motivational work environment are all keys to success. Assembling a quality team is very important. Their effective and efficient execution is critical. But sustainability is paramount to your ultimate long-term success.

Some examples of directing activities include:

- Implementing your own leadership (see Chapter 2) and management styles (see Chapter 9).
- Coaching and Mentoring (see Chapter 4).
- Operational decision-making and RAPID tool (see Chapter 12).

- Implementing Growth Drivers (see Chapter 13).
- Managing the 4 Ps (see Chapter 15).

Control

> **Lessons Learned**
>
> I have always requested my teams create CEO dashboards or one-time "snapshot" reports to help me monitor many KPIs, such as daily revenues, sales prospect pipelines, new product updates, top ten customers by revenues, average contract values (top to bottom), sales cycle trends, social media activities and click through rates (CTRs), ROI on marketing spend, and recently lost business to name a few. Above are the more frequently monitored metrics, but it goes without saying that other key financial reports and analyses are created on a monthly and quarterly basis as well.

This function involves monitoring and reporting on all activities to ensure compliance with and completion of your plans. Being results-driven takes this process a step further by tracking output through KPIs based on progress toward quantified achievement of corporate, team, and individual goals. An internal comparison of actual results and targets is a useful view to take. This allows for proactive and corrective measures to be put into place where warranted. These performance measures allow for better decision-making.

Some examples of control (monitoring and reporting) activities include:

- Budgeting of financials and operational plans (see Chapter 14,).
- Setting financial KPIs (see Chapter 14) and CSAT metrics (see Chapter 6).

- Financial Statement Analysis (see Chapter 14).

To be successfully executed, many business activities cut across and are included in all four management functions, of Planning, Organizing, Directing and Control. These need to be planned, created, resourced, executed, and monitored. Examples of a few of these activities include:

- Creating and delivering your Mission statement (see Chapter 4).
- Creating and delivering your Strategic Intent (see Chapter 5).
- The Sales Management activities (see Chapter 16).

What are your thoughts?

List your own personal management practices and behaviors (and those of your boss) that best lead to organizational success. Are there some others that have negative impacts (what are they and their results)?

Based on the three styles of learning theory, which approach do you find the most comfortable and effective?

List the five to ten top skills effective managers must possess. How many of these do you share and put into regular use?

Which of the four management functions is your strong point and which could be improved (and why)?

CHAPTER 9

Management Styles

Chapter Preview

- **When and why each of the fifteen management styles should be practiced and what are the pros and cons of each**

- **Choose the style(s) that best fits your personality and comfort levels.**

- **The styles that are best when addressing conflict.**

Just as with leaders, managers have numerous styles at their disposal to interact with their subordinates at the workplace. Deciding which style is best for you depends on numerous factors, including your personality, skill set, experience as well as your team's mindset, level of skills, needs, and the organizational work culture. Showing flexibility and being adaptive to your changing internal and external environments are also strong management traits for planning, organizing, delegating, and making decisions to fulfill organizational goals.

Many, but not all, of the styles I will present below are similar to the leadership styles discussed in Chapter 2. While the styles may be similar, the situations and precedents as to why a specific style is deployed may be different. Thus, these styles warrant further discussion from a managerial perspective due to their importance in either making or breaking an individual manager as well as their organization's ultimate success. These styles include:

Autocratic

This is a top-down, one-way approach with tightly defined parameters. The manager holds all the power and involves absolute authoritarian control over their staff. Staff questions are discouraged, and no time is given to staff development. A strict hierarchy and reporting structure is established, including a clear vision and direction being set from the top with strong control and decision-making mechanisms in place. In today's work environment, the potential benefits of this style are minimal and suspect, and will likely be short-lived if ever deployed. Thus, I do not recommend this management style.

Authoritative

This type of management dictates exactly what is required, and staff are then expected to follow such orders. It is synonymous to the autocratic style. This style lends its way to micromanaging staff, which can lead to a higher rate of turnover. Those who do not comply may be punished. Usually, innovation is stifled and inefficiencies remain. This style works best if a manager needs to make quick or urgent decisions in a crisis mode and the staff are inexperienced. It is useful when there is little room for mistakes (e.g., military operations, construction sites, etc.). It may also be utilized in business settings when a mission needs to be executed flawlessly. Once the team gains more experience and expertise, most leaders transition to a more amenable approach.

Persuasive

This style is utilized within a hierarchical structure and requires managers to convince their teams that the decisions made are good for them. It is more prominent in non-Western cultures when the manager has much more experience than their staff. While more trust should be built through persuasion than dictatorial orders, this is still a top-down approach. Employees are still restricted as little to no feedback is requested from them. If this style persists, employees may become very dependent on their manager.

Paternalistic

This style centers on creating a family-like work environment where policies implemented are in the best interest and benefit of staff. Managers expect their staff's trust and loyalty in return. While employees may feel more attached and loyal, the manager still makes unilateral decisions, and no collaboration is present or any requests for staff input are made.

Democratic

This style encourages staff input and idea-sharing during the decision-making process. The manager must possess good communications skills to lead such a process. The majority rules here and the most popular idea usually wins. But the manager still has the final say. This style may lead to inefficiencies due to staff mulling over options for too long when trying to build consensus. However, this is a very popular managerial style.

Consultative

This approach is taken when the manager is surrounded by a team of highly specialized experts. Opinions are sought with the goal of gaining consensus as the staff possesses more expertise than the manager leading them. This approach should lead to more idea-sharing, innovation, and problem-solving. On the downside, this is a very time-intensive process for the manager to undertake and, as the team is continuously asked to solve problems, some resentment could result if individuals feel their ideas are not truly being considered or the manager is taking credit for them.

Participative

Here, staff are given more information to work with and everyone is involved in the decision-making process. The manager seeks staff's thoughts, ideas, and opinions. While staff may feel more engaged, this process can be very slow and arduous. At times, the "squeakiest wheel" takes over the floor. This style is better suited in situations where a major change in direction is needed and there is also strong resistance.

Collaborative

This style encourages an open forum of communication. Staff take ownership, but the majority still rules. This process can also be time-consuming, and the best decisions are not always reached. This style is useful to foster innovation, engagement, and mutual trust.

Visionary

This style requires an inspirational and charismatic manager (traits of an effective leader) who is firm, yet fair, and focused on staff motivation, alignment, and calculated risk-taking to deliver on the vision. Explaining "the why" is important to staff. A high degree of EI (see Chapter 3) on the part of the manager is also necessary. Managers who utilize this approach are not usually very detail-oriented or hands-on. Thus, their teams need to be experienced and self-directed. This style usually leads to high staff satisfaction, engagement, and low turnover. If you possess the management skills to execute this approach, it comes highly recommended.

Transformational

This style is witnessed more in fast-paced industries such as hi-tech, where external change is dominant and continuous. Agility, flexibility, and adaptability are required on the part of the manager and staff. Thinking "outside the box" is encouraged and the performance bar is always being raised. Such high-pressure environments may sometimes lead to staff burnout, which needs continuous monitoring. But this is a very useful style to deploy in driving organizational change and staff behaviors.

Coaching

Also known as the servient style, it includes a heavy dose of coaching, training, teaching, and mentoring on the part of the manager. It is a useful style when the goal is to build and promote from within vs. recruiting externally. The manager is more of an advisor than an enforcer. Strong interpersonal skills, ethics, and trust must be apparent, as well as EI skills. The manager guides and develops their team. This results in strong employee bonds being established. Learning from mistakes instead of being disciplined or punished is the norm. The downsides of this approach include:

- The manager not always being as visible as needed due to being occupied by numerous one-on-one coaching sessions.

- Most negative or unhappy employees do not benefit from coaching.

- Being more long-term focused may cause the manager to lose sight of shorter-term objectives.

- Staff may begin to think business results and output are secondary to their personal and professional growth.

This approach focuses on staff and has a lesser focus on financial results. It is not highly recommended as a holistic approach but should be used when an ideal staff developmental situation presents itself.

Laissez-Faire

A manager pursuing this style is very hands-off and provides little staff oversight or supervision and reluctantly steps in only when asked to do so. Thus, the staff should be experienced and self-motivated as they may see their manager only at the beginning and end of most processes. It is somewhat safe to say that, while creativity and innovation may be sparked through staff empowerment, the manager usually contributes very little. This style has a reputation of being the least effective. I agree.

Delegative

Here, the manager assigns tasks and empowers the staff to execute. The manager then evaluates the output and makes suggestions for improvements. Employee satisfaction levels from this approach run high, except for those needing more direction. Dealing with conflict resolution utilizing this style may also lead to problems. This style suits managers who have limited expertise themselves, are in a decentralized structure, and possess numerous SMEs (subject matter experts) on their team.

Transactional

The driver of this style is utilizing rewards and recognition (R&R) to achieve stronger results. These rewards are extrinsic in nature and are not typically seen by staff as being as "favorable" as receiving intrinsic rewards. Extrinsic rewards are tangible and physically presented for accomplishing a positive result. Examples include plaques, trophies, bonuses, etc. While intrinsic rewards are intangible and come from within the individual. It's their inner knowledge that they have done something right. Examples include a positive inner feeling of happiness, self-worth, and fulfillment. This management style is characterized by the terms "pay for performance" and "piece-work pay" with the latter term and process coming under much scrutiny. If this style is deployed, it should only be utilized over short time periods. While R&R sounds great in principle, it is short-lived and not highly recommended.

Pacesetting

Here, the manager sets the pace and leads from the front of the pack, being a Jack Welch of sorts. [6] Objectives are set high and difficult to reach, which can lead to staff burnout and failure if they are not totally capable of executing. As individual performance is recognized and rewarded, staff resentment can also occur. This style has its useful moments and should not be prevailing over the long term.

Lessons Learned

How managers deal with conflict is a topic I have yet to touch on in detail. A number of managerial styles can be exhibited based on the situation at hand. First, I view the situation's severity (ranging from petty issues to more serious risks) and who is involved (based on their maturity level and rank within our organization). I have dealt with varying conflicts differently. Styles I have exhibited include:

- Avoiding the situation and letting it work its way out (laissez-faire).

- Suggesting a compromise solution (coaching).

- Being accommodating and putting the team's issues first (democratic).

- Searching for a win-win resolution (collaborative).

- In extreme situations, I have been known to take an authoritative stance, "digging in" and not giving up at all costs. I only use this style when I know that giving in will lead to serious and detrimental consequences.

> ### Lessons Learned
>
> I favor being democratic and participative, but rely heavily on the art of persuasion. I can be hands-on when it comes to coaching practices, but can also be delegative and empowering when my team has earned my trust. I support the use of best practices and I am a big supporter of transformational change management. I also thoroughly enjoy being "visionary" when the opportunity presents itself.
>
> As you can probably tell, I tend to adapt my management style based on the business circumstances and whom I am working with (my individual team members). You will recall that this "situational" style is similar to how I address my leadership challenges.

What are your thoughts?

What is the management style of your boss? Is it effective (why and why not)?

What are the most prominent and effective management styles you exhibit, and would your colleagues, friends, and loved ones agree?

Is there a style you do not utilize that might benefit others (which ones and why)?

What situational criteria do you consider when possibly changing to another style?

CHAPTER 10

Management Attributes

Chapter Preview

- **Key personal attributes, traits, and aptitudes shared by successful managers.**
- **Where and how to improve your business acumen and performance results**
- **How to reduce or eliminate the pitfalls of poor Stakeholder Management, Performance Management, and Time Management**
- **Tips to becoming a more effective negotiator.**

Successful managers possess and exhibit many of the same personal attributes and traits. These set them apart from more mediocre managers. Their most useful and impactful attributes include:

Communication

Verbal and nonverbal (i.e., written) communication skills should be utilized and enhanced on a continuous basis at all levels within your organization. Methods of delivery to explore include one-on-one meetings, interactive team sessions, company-wide townhalls with a question and answer (Q&A) session, weekly CEO email updates, newsletters, posters with key organizational messages, and utilization of your intranet for engaged colleagues to share information, insights, and success stories.

When making formal presentations, I find the fewer the slides and the fewer the words on them, the better. Just include your key talking points on the slide and speak about them. Avoid reading slides to your audience. Boring! You want the audience's attention focused on you and your message, not on the screen or their smartphones. Once you have the audience's full attention, remember the importance of speaking with emotion, using voice inflections and positive body language. Always be prepared and practice beforehand.

I find the use of sharing personal stories and anecdotes to be a much more effective approach to engage an audience than just sharing facts. Everyone enjoys a good story. Remember the adage "Say what you mean and mean what you say," as many audiences can see through disingenuousness. Try and create a dialogue with your audience. This can be achieved by asking the audience a series of intriguing and compelling questions throughout your presentation, actively listening to their input, and then responding back to them when appropriate. Sometimes effective listening can be more important than what you say.

A simple presentation format can be to briefly communicate what you plan to share with the audience, share your message, and then close with a reminder of the highlights of key takeaways of what you shared.

Acronyms are abbreviated terms usually formed from the initial letters or syllables of a group of words that make up a name or title. Be careful with your use of acronyms, which are used worldwide in most industries. While each industry has its own set of acronyms that everyone in that industry should know, listeners from other industries may have difficulty understanding. The effective use of acronyms can be very beneficial and efficient, and shows the speaker's knowledge, understanding, or expertise of the topic at hand. However, they can be confusing to some less-experienced audience members, as everyone comes to a presentation with varying levels of knowledge and understanding of the topic. Only a few, brave audience members will ever speak up and ask, "What does that acronym stand for?" Most of the others will sit in silence, having no clue as to its meaning. If the meaning is not clear, many in the audience will unfortunately "tune out" of the presentation or be distracted as they Google the acronym's meaning on their smartphones. As a presenter, a foolproof way to avoid losing a portion of your audience's attention is to show (on your slide) the full definition of the acronym. While this suggestion sounds so simple, many presenters still do not heed this advice.

Lessons Learned

When I was a senior executive sponsor for one of my organization's leadership development programs, I usually sponsored four teams a year. This program ran for six consecutive years and was one of my favorite activities.

Each team was comprised of a coach and approximately ten "up-and-coming" team members selected by our senior management. The program ran for a two-to-three-month duration. One of the many program outcomes was the selection, execution, and final presentation of an internal project being proposed to bring new efficiencies and productivity improvements to our staff. Little to no additional costs were to be incurred to implement the projects. At the program's culmination, individual team presentations were made to our senior management and the projects were either agreed upon to move forward or terminated at that time.

There was a lot of credibility at stake here as we were competing with nine other teams. I always told my teams, upfront, that this presentation was critical to get right. Thus, they would need to plan at least three rehearsals in front of me. They could, of course, rehearse on their own as well. They were always very surprised by my request for making what they assumed was a simple fifteen-minute presentation.   *(continued)*

When the first rehearsal began, each team usually presented at least twenty to thirty slides full of paragraphs of details. They read like a book, which was information overload, considering we had only fifteen minutes (including a critical five-minute Q&A conclusion). I suggested cut after painful cut with a rationale to back up my reductions. Usually, I just said, "So what" or asked, "Why is this point important?" They reluctantly agreed to my suggested changes.

By the time our third rehearsal was completed, each team's slide deck was usually no more than five slides (with bullet points and no complete sentences). The teams were very happy at the end of this arduous process. All presentations went over well and were approved by senior management. When making presentations, attention to detail wins out.

Lessons Learned

One of best examples of a success story related to communication was my creation of an interactive session I termed "Huddle with Hubble." These were held weekly when my travel schedule permitted and involved a small group of randomly selected colleagues (twelve to fifteen names were pulled out of a hat) from all departments and divisions.

I would set the tone and purpose of these sessions upfront. I had the participants briefly introduce themselves and their roles (two minutes each). I would then begin asking them questions. They came prepared as the attendees knew my expectations and the questions in advance through the agenda included with the RSVP invitation. An example of a question was "What is the greatest challenge or barrier you face in successfully executing your job?" We ended each session with a roundtable discussion enabling participants to ask me any question on their mind.

The takeaways and benefits from our 1.5 hours together were many. For example, I befriended many colleagues I did not know well, just as they did with me and their peers in attendance. I was able to share my personal views as to our business aspirations and gain their insights. Lastly, those around the table were able to make meaningful recommendations to resolve many of their peers' job challenges or barriers.

After each session, I sent out a simple email evaluation form with a few questions to rate the session's value and offer input as to how we may improve future "Huddles." The feedback was very positive and useful.

"Huddle with Hubble" became so popular (through attendee word of mouth) that others who had not attended yet sought me out to ask when they would be invited. Those who did attend would ask me when they would be invited a second time. Nice!

Lessons Learned

As previously mentioned, the art of storytelling is a great way to capture your audience's attention and interest. Sharing your personal vulnerabilities in this way will only make you appear more human to your colleagues.

Networking

People prefer to do business with those they know, trust, and enjoy being around. Having a strong and growing contact list is also a great recruiting tool to bring talent to your organization or find your next workplace. Making a conscious effort to regularly keep in touch with your network is an important, best practice. Such informal interactions that begin as a personal gesture of just reaching out can often lead to relevant information gathering or uncovering new business or personal opportunities. Not taking advantage of the latest social media tools is a missed opportunity for networking vs. solely relying on your phone.

Stakeholder Management

This skill is totally underrated, yet so important. It is about the art of persuasion and influencing others to support you, your ideas, and future actions. There are three main groups of stakeholders you need to influence: your supervisor (upwards), your peers (across), and your direct reports (downward). All three are equally important to your success.

Ensure you add other stakeholders to your short list from outside these three groups, such as Corporate Services colleagues (e.g., Finance, IT, Legal, Procurement, Human Resources). Your primary stakeholders may inevitably go to their Corporate Services colleagues to seek specific expert advice. You will want to have already influenced these experts yourself as well.

Managing your stakeholders is a continuous process. Even if they support you, you should periodically check back with them as things can change. The best compliment you can receive is that colleagues support your ideas or your proposal, not because of a reporting relationship but because they believe in you.

> **Lessons Learned**
>
> Sometimes, who you know is just as important than what you know. Name dropping does work to "get in the door." Given the choice, I prefer to work with friends vs. strangers. But I am always willing to meet new friends.

> **Lessons Learned**
>
> Avoid alienating anyone during your stakeholder management process. Unfortunately, some stakeholders possess big egos, thin skins, and may bring corporate politics into the mix. If any of them feel neglected, your chances of success will be seriously compromised. Never wait until the last minute to meet with a key stakeholder, as they may become defensive in believing you truly do not want their "valuable" insights, but just their "rubber stamp" approval.

Most "C-suite" level leaders are very busy and do not have a lot of free time to give you when you are seeking buy-in on new project proposals. The most efficient method to gain stakeholder support is achieved by identifying what excites them concerning your proposal and, more importantly, where they have specific concerns. Your primary purpose is to question them to gain these insights. What you think is important to them is irrelevant. Thus, refrain from giving a sales pitch. To gain approval, your proposal must satisfactorily address the stakeholder's interests and concerns or you will have missed the boat.

Lessons Learned

Delivering great financial results is obviously very important. But if you achieve your targets while alienating your boss, not involving them or not allowing them to share in your victories, your success may be overlooked or not appreciated for its true worth and contribution. This may end with a win/loss scenario (good results, but no recognition, appreciation or accolades). A painful lesson to learn.

Lessons Learned

To improve the quality of your interactions with "C-suite" leaders, master the two-minute elevator pitch. Focus on:
- "Why" something needs to be done (what the benefits will be).
- "Who" will perform it.
- "What" will be done and by when.
- "What" ultimate success will look like.

Avoid details about the "how" (process).

Performance Management

Performance management entails a comprehensive process and tools to manage, develop, evaluate, measure, and coach your people to achieve organizational, departmental, and individual goals and performance targets. The main goal of performance management is to increase the competencies and capabilities of your staff through time, resources, and investment. In doing so, an expectation of exceeding organizational targets is not an unreasonable request.

You want to create a work environment where staff can perform at their best by delivering quality output with efficiency and effectiveness. This can be enabled by implementing a communication-based process of continuous collaboration between management and staff.

Performance management is usually executed at two levels:

- Strategic (plans at the corporate level)

- Administrative or Operational (plans at the departmental level)

- Problems that may contribute to poor performance management processes include:

- A lack of consistency and/or credibility on the part of management

- Providing mixed signals in your feedback to staff

- A lack of trust between management and staff

- A lack of established goals or they become moving targets

To avoid these common pitfalls, the following step-by-step process should be implemented:

- **Planning**—Define each role with a detailed job description with SMART objectives (see Chapter 2), with defined goals, performance plans, and metrics for tracking progress. These should be agreed upon between the manager and employee.

- **Coaching**—Regularly provide guidance and training, which should be a positive exchange and experience. Such training usually addresses technical "hard skills" related to the actual work itself, but "soft skills" should also be included.

- **Reviewing**—This involves the performance appraisal (PA) process itself of providing feedback on employee performance to date. While quantifiable outcomes are important, this is also an ideal time to discuss personal behaviors and corporate values. While PA reviews are normally completed annually, the more frequent, the better. Formal quarterly reviews are best, but with informal daily interactions as they may occur. Every interaction can be an opportunity for learning. If this collaborative interactive method is used, there should never be any year-end surprises. Longer term career development and succession planning should also be addressed when applicable. Thoughts of any possible changes to next year's plan should be laid out at this time.

- **Action**—This involved establishing and implementing a reward and recognition plan during the compensation phase after the PA process is concluded.

Lessons Learned

I prefer to conduct PAs on a quarterly basis as priorities and objectives may need to be adjusted, changed, reset, reprioritized, or cancelled. Communication with staff should be continuous between your quarterly updates. You must make the time for this important activity and staff exchange. Many managers find it difficult to deliver bad or negative reviews, which in truth is a disservice to their underperforming staff.

Lessons Learned

When my direct reportees think they are performing much better than I perceive, I ask them to share why they feel as they do and provide me with concrete examples. Thus, they must "talk their way up" vs. me "talking them down." Usually, if my assessment of their performance is correct and I have not missed important results on their part, they struggle to come up with strong examples, yet can become very defensive if I do the same. I have been known to change my preliminary PA ratings based on good evidence provided. This transparent and fair interactive process usually ends with a win-win compromise and learning experience.

Lessons Learned

I have utilized many PA software rating tools and have yet to discover the perfect one that is fully embraced by my teams. Experience has shown me that employees who are rated high tend to like the tool, while those who do not, usually complain. It is usually not the tool's fault. Instead of focusing on a tool, I focus on coaching my direct reportees to embrace and follow the performance management steps outlined above. I also reinforce the need for them to exhibit empathy, fairness, transparency, and candor with their own teams.

Lessons Learned

I support utilizing a "360-degree" component as part of each PA by sharing relevant, yet anonymous, insights from peers and direct reports. This approach can be useful in reinforcing the reviewee's key learning points. I created my own 360-degree tool (with my HR department's support) as my direct reports were constantly rating themselves as a "role model" (in their self-appraisals) related to their leadership and management abilities. They seldom chose "satisfactorily meets requirements" or even more rarely "needs development." During our PA, I showed them

Those being promoted from within possess a proven track record that you have witnessed firsthand rather than having to rely mainly on someone's CV (resume) and your interviewing acumen and skills. Mutual trust with internal recruits should already be established. Only when a new skill set that we do not possess internally and is urgently needed, will I go outside. In most instances, I will compare external candidates against internal ones to ensure professional, fair, and equitable staffing policies are being followed. Of course, hiring new blood (i.e., gaining new perspectives and a diversity of views) can be a good thing as well.

Lessons Learned

Related to recruiting, all things being equal, I am a big supporter of promoting from within. This approach reinforces your organization's career development and succession planning and rewards results. It also allows you to continue building staff loyalty and commitment. Internal recruiting is seen as less risky, as they are well known to your organization. External recruits have no internal track record and usually have a steep learning curve to overcome to understand your corporate structure, culture, and their new colleagues (i.e., who does what, where to go to find what they need, how decisions are made), just to name a few challenges facing new staff. However, these challenges and more can be addressed and overcome by establishing a strong new employee orientation and indoctrination (onboarding) program.

Time Management

To quote Elon Musk, "If you give yourself thirty days to clean your home, it will take you thirty days. But if you give yourself three hours, it will take three hours. The same applies to your goals, ambitions and potential." In other words, tasks and activities are completed within the timeline you set for them. Be efficient and productive with your time, as it is one of your most valuable assets. Managing it well is a skill that most high achievers possess. However, the key is to not just manage time, but to manage yourself. This is less about how hard you work and more about how smartly you work. Focus on what you want to achieve (the output or expected results) and not on the activity to achieve the result. You will want to work fast and efficiently, but not be in a hurry. Once you give your time away, you will never get that time back.

> **Lessons Learned**
>
> Building a checklist of tasks to be achieved may be a useful method to organize your activities. But refrain from focusing first on the more simple, less valuable tasks as the more complex and value-add items will just keep getting pushed out to a later day. While your task list may be reduced, your true contributions are diminished.

Many benefits can be gained from perfecting this skill set. These include freeing up more of your time, improving your chances for greater success, better prioritization of work and stress relief. On the other hand, not practicing good time management techniques can lead to time wastage, missing key goals, poor quality output, higher stress levels, and damage to your reputation.

Success can be achieved by proactively planning, organizing, and controlling your time spent on all activities (including project management) to increase your effectiveness, efficiency, and productivity. It can assist you in establishing the correct work-life balance as well.

Lessons Learned

In the office, I practice an "open door" policy. To successfully achieve this requires me to utilize simple, proven, yet tough, time management tactics, such as:

- Schedule meetings in your colleague's office, so you can get up and leave when you wish.
- Clarify the topic's importance and urgency before accepting someone's meeting request.
- Before accepting a meeting, ask: "Does the issue need to be resolved today, this week, or this month?" "Is the meeting to brainstorm or just a social catch-up visit?" Clarifying this will dictate how soon you need to get together.
- Screen your phone calls as many colleagues will not leave a message, but keep calling back until you answer. My experience shows that most of these are usually not important or urgent.

Keep in mind, most colleagues want physical "face time" with you instead over the phone, email, or text messages. Therefore, try to avoid the "fly-bys" who quickly and unexpectedly enter your office and sit down. If possible, try to greet them at your door first and answer their question or resolve their issue standing up. It will take less time. If they do sit down, you should simply stand up when you want to end the impromptu discussion, alerting them that you need to leave. If they forget their manners and people skills and do not follow your lead, as a last resort, walk out of your office. While this may sound a little harsh, trust me, they will soon follow you.

Without prioritization, you may complete various tasks, but they may result in lesser valued outputs.

A simple method to address your priorities is to categorize and rank them. Tackle high importance, high urgency initiatives first. Then, set hard deadlines for high importance, but less urgent initiatives. As to tasks of lower importance, but higher urgency, these should be delegated to other colleagues you trust. Being comfortable with delegation can be one of your best high-leverage activities as it frees you up to focus on more important activities. Lastly, for less important and less urgent tasks categorized as repetitive "busy work," try to cluster or combine these efforts together when addressing them. You must also learn to become comfortable saying "NO" to less important tasks as well. Be polite and professional, but firm.

Learning how to multitask can pay you big dividends, but always allow adequate blocks of uninterrupted time for strategic and creative thinking. Try not to allow your underperformers or your most vocal "squeaky wheel" colleagues to take all your time away from spending it with your top performers and future stars, as they need your time as well. Lastly, to manage your own time well, set your own schedule and do not allow others to take over your agenda.

> **Lessons Learned**
>
> Remember Pareto's 80/20 Principle, that 20 percent of inputs bring 80 percent of results. This can be true for financial results as well as people. Identifying the "20-percenters" is the true challenge.

Negotiating

Having good negotiating skills is an attribute that can pay managers huge dividends if they perfect them. Negotiating involves the qualities of discussing, bargaining, and persuading others to reach an agreement or solution.

Strong negotiators possess skills in communicating and identifying nonverbal cues, being interactive, regularly asking for feedback, and being influential. Good negotiators plan and strategize beforehand and always have a backup plan to consider other possible and acceptable alternatives. If you are not happy or comfortable with the proposed outcomes, know when to walk away. Do not use this as a negotiation ploy or threat, unless you are serious about doing it. If not, you will look foolish coming back again.

> **Lessons Learned**
>
> A large customer had a contract dispute with us and was refusing to extend our agreement to our newly updated service. They had the right to terminate the agreement and we were obligated to return all prior payments (worth million dollars). This horrible contract needed to be addressed urgently. I met with their decision-maker who was a very professional and logical person. We both agreed on a list of five issues needing our attention. I asked him to list these in order of his priorities while I did the same. As we compared each other's lists, his top three were my least important ones and vice versa. We quickly noticed that we were not that far off as to addressing each other's top priorities. We discussed each of our lists and came to an agreement for new contractual terms, as I easily agreed to his priorities and he to mine. For example, he wanted to be locked into "fair market" pricing, which I could concede in return for a longer term five-year extension which he accepted. All other priorities ended in similar fashion. We both went home winners.

When negotiating, it is not uncommon to concede or "give in" on certain points as you work through a laundry list of issues. However, always reserve the right to hold off on these being "final." Instead, leave them as "contingent" upon all other issues being resolved amicably. Otherwise, you may agree on their main issues while yours go unresolved. It may be difficult to put their issues back on the table once they think you have already signed off on them.

Other negotiating tips include:

- Practicing with "role playing" beforehand
- Doing your research and being prepared
- Building rapport first

- Not taking things personally
- Knowing your final goals
- Having a willingness to compromise
- Knowing your own weaknesses
- Offering multiple approaches to resolving potential objections
- Enforcing time restrictions for a final decision

Lessons Learned

Related to pricing, I have two short negotiation stories to share.

Short Story #1

Some of the most difficult and challenging negotiations I have dealt with involved pricing. In many instances, the prospect started our discussion by stating, "Your prices are too high." In my view, this was a distraction ploy, which I did not "bite on" or justify by being defensive. Instead, I reminded them that we had not even agreed upon the exact service they were going to purchase nor its price. I asked them to clarify to me the budget they had to spend. Then, I could customize a package to meet their pricing requirements.

I also told them I was our decision-maker. Therefore, I could strike a final deal that day. Was I dealing with their decision-maker? The answer was "no." Thus, I knew any concessions I would have agreed to in this meeting would be expanded later by the real decision-maker. I told them I was wasting my time. Their decision-maker eventually joined our meeting and shared their budget with me (low-balling it, of course). I offered a few compelling options for them to choose from. They eventually spent more than the original budget shared with me to get the level of service they truly wanted.

Short Story #2

Do not ever overinflate your "list pricing" too much in the hopes that you will look good later by drastically lowering it. This occurred to me once when our sales rep did so against my better judgement. Once he dropped the pricing, the prospect was tremendously insulted. We lost our credibility and his trust, resulting in NO deal!

What are your thoughts?

What are the most important attributes successful managers possess, and do you also share these?

Are there specific attributes you should improve or add (why)?

What are some best practices you utilize to maximize your network and relationships?

Can you benefit from practicing better stakeholder management skills in managing up, across, and downwards within your organization (where and why)?

Is your Performance Management process understood and accepted by management and staff? Where can improvements be made and in which of the four steps?

List your top five current Time Management techniques and what new ones might you explore?

Can your negotiation skills be improved (where and how)?

CHAPTER 11

Management Work Environment

Chapter Preview

- Building awareness of business fundamentals "out of your control."

- How to proactively influence the most important business fundamentals "within your control"

- Addressing internal work environment challenges facing managers today.

- Unique characteristics common within high-performance teams.

- Steps and actions taken to improve team performance levels.

- Approaches and actions to become more strategically focused.

- Proven strategies to build a competitive advantage.

Managing a work environment successfully can be quite challenging and complex. This encompasses everything from people and talent management to building high-performance teams. Strategies must be formulated, yet the daily operations of all business functions must also run smoothly. Focus must center on delivering solid financial results (e.g., driving profitable growth), but other nonfinancial factors cannot be overlooked such as the creation of a safe, healthy, and appealing workplace. In this chapter, we will focus on people and strategies while providing examples of "how to" excel.

Business Fundamentals

As a manager, you have a myriad of functions and activities that need to be executed flawlessly if you are to be successful. If you do not understand these, even at a basic level, you are flying blind. A higher level of knowledge is recommended though. Otherwise, you will not have a firm grasp of your business drivers. These are the levers to pull or activate through implementation of specific actions and initiatives to sustain financial success. There are two categories of these business fundamentals:

Uncontrollable External Dynamics—Also referred to as the "Circle of Concern," these are driven by market trends, competitive landscapes, currency fluctuations, unexpected lawsuits, political and civil unrest, war, pandemics, technological innovations, natural disasters, and economic factors like Gross Domestic Product (GDP), inflation, and unemployment rates. While you cannot control these from occurring, taking proactive and preventative measures to build greater awareness of the likelihood of where and how they might impact your organization is smart business. It is very important to have a Business Continuity Plan (BCP) to provide contingencies as to what you will do if you face one or more of these scenarios.

One logical step is establishing a Risk Management Committee (RMC) within your organization made up of senior leaders. A quarterly meeting should be held to monitor, revise and add new risks to be monitored, tracked, reduced, or eliminated. Operational (controllable) risks (see below) should also be included within your monitoring and tracking process. These risks are included as part of your normal business activities.

Most low-to-medium business risks should be managed by each responsible department as part of their daily operations. The risks requiring the most attention are those categorized as "significant." These are defined by the possibility or likelihood of them occurring and their financial fallout and/or brand damage to your organization being "high."

Controllable External Dynamics—Also referred to as the "Circle of Influence," these are factors that can be proactively addressed and manipulated by your team's direct actions on a regular basis. I will address the areas that are vital to any business' longevity and sustainability. These areas necessitate taking a continuous "pulse" to monitor progress and ensure seamless execution. In doing so, I suggest the creation of a simple "Management Checklist" to keep the following issues in the forefront of your thoughts and actions. Manage these activities well and you will win.

From a commercial standpoint, driving profitable and sustainable growth is a major priority. This process starts with a focus on your topline (revenue) growth. Managing your cost base is also fiscally responsible. But, as Jeremy Corbyn said, "You grow your way to prosperity; you don't cut your way to it." Becoming more efficient, effective, and productive is very important, but without growth, having these traits becomes a moot point. Managing both revenues and expenses will help ensure your topline growth is more profitable.

Other key business fundamentals that need continuous attention through the formulation of a logical and comprehensive blueprint of operations include:

- **People**—Taking care of your number one asset, your people talent. A motivated and happy team leads to happy customers. Continuously strive to improve your internal work environment while training and developing staff. Focus first on your staff's alignment, development, and skill sets.

- **Value**—Creating value within your portfolio of products and services that customers are willing to purchase. Their perceptions are what matter. This is your endless mission.

- **Strategy**—Prioritizing your strategic focus and business development planning processes and putting these execution plans into action. Monitor and tweak regularly.

- **Priority**—Making the necessary tradeoffs and displacements according to your available bandwidth, as everyone can only pursue so much. This strategy involves deciding what you are not going to do.

- **Finance**—Securing the necessary financing to fund your organization, focusing on cash generation. No money, no business. But maintain your financial freedom; it is that simple.

- **Accounting**—Implementing appropriate accounting practices for tracking and reporting purposes utilizing appropriate KPIs. Adapt to adverse situations with decisiveness and speed. No negative surprises are welcomed here.

- **Operations**—Ensuring efficient operations are in place (e.g., infrastructure, systems, processes) to run the business. Become efficient and agile.

- **Promotion**—Making concerted efforts in sales, marketing, and branding to attract and secure new business and retaining existing customers. Strive to achieve brand resonance.

- **Customer**—Implementing a CX plan, including all customer touch points. Train and educate all staff on the importance of CX. Customer loyalty is number one factor in terms of driving sustainable profits.

Work Environment

While leaders play a key role in creating a motivational work environment, managers can assist here as well. Our workforce continues to change and is becoming younger. Managing through this multi-generational work environment is now the norm. We are facing a "talent cliff." As baby boomers are getting closer to retirement, a new set of millennial leaders and managers will need to be developed. Diversity, ethnicity, gender equality, and inclusion need to be a big part of all staff planning.

Staff demands and interests are ever-changing and increasing. New sets of demands are evolving that require managers to successfully operate differently. Remote and geographically dispersed project teams have become the new normal. Telecommuting is occurring regularly and can be cost-effective and satisfying for staff. But it is not ideal for every position or person.

Hybrid and virtual work models (the mixing of onsite and remote staff) are presenting a new set of challenges that managers must quickly address. This point is reinforced by a recent study conducted by McKinsey. They found that nine out of ten organizations polled,

> **Lessons Learned**
>
> Organizations can function effectively and efficiently if they are adaptive. Hybrid work environments have become the new normal. No stone should be left unturned as to what is best for your staff and organization. When considering such hybrid models, each functional role and individual should be assessed independently as to their work options as this is not a one size fits all situation. A new priority is to ensure working remotely from home does not become a detriment to financial results, staff health and well-being, etc. A goal for managers should be to utilize this opportunity to create a better, higher quality employee work experience and engagement. Doing so should drive greater performance and staff retention.

stating they were actively utilizing or planning to experiment with such hybrid workplace models.

Before implementing such new models, many questions come to mind to carefully think through and address beforehand. There is no single or correct answer to these questions, as each organization must do what is best for their situation and staff. Some questions to ask yourself include:

- How will the manager and staff effectively interact and communicate?
- How will newly recruited staff be efficiently onboarded (orientations, training)?
- Does existing performance measures need to be rethought or new ones created?
- How will social cohesion of staff and a unified virtual corporate culture be maintained?
- Does the traditional workspace setting need to be reconfigured?
- What tools and technologies are best to allow for remote connection of teams (e.g., video conferencing, messaging)?
- What new work processes, policies, and related corporate guidelines should be created and communicated in support of these to ensure all aspects are addressed from a technological, safety, security, and staff health and well-being perspective?

Building High-Performance Teams

High-performing teams are a powerful organizational resource that needs a strong manager who "walks the talk," and is a source of team inspiration, energy, and enthusiasm. The team's makeup can include remote staff, freelancers and colleagues at varying locations. Possessing diverse expertise and complementary skill sets will help you outperform your goals and overachieve expected results. Your team will need careful development and nurturing to bring out the right behaviors and actions.

While a team's size may vary, researchers state that a high-performing team's composition on average should be no less than six members and no more than ten. [38] Smaller teams can experience bandwidth issues while larger teams may struggle with team member ability to have an equal voice and can negatively affect decision-making. Try to avoid extreme membership levels within your team's makeup. Success is all about the quality of your team members. Quality outweighs quantity.

How do you go about building a high-performance team? This process starts with recruiting the "right" people talent. As the legendary NBA Hall of Famer Michael Jordon put it, "Talent wins games, but teamwork and intelligence wins championships."

A big component of your team's composition should include cultural diversity and team members who share mutual trust. Such trust can be established in many ways, including one-on-one interactions or by various outdoor or offsite teambuilding activities. Teambuilding activities, while sometimes sound childish, can work well to build comradery. These offsite events are good to rework the team's mindset. There are numerous qualified organizations that are well prepared to customize, coordinate, and facilitate such activities to your team's needs. Seeking outside assistance for the planning and execution of such teambuilding activities is highly recommended.

Once mutual trust is established, your team should be ready to align themselves around a clear and unified purpose of what they are trying to achieve and setting individual and team goals to be measured against. These goals should be consequential to have meaning.

Creating a Team Charter is another logical step. It is a written document that encompasses your team's purpose and goals. It also elaborates on how the team plans to work together (i.e., operating rules, roles, acceptable behaviors, values).

One individual should be assigned by management or voted to lead their team members. This individual needs to possess both the accountability to lead as well as the authority to do so. In addition, the team leader is responsible for providing individual and team development where and when needed.

The leader should avoid micromanaging unless the team is struggling or floundering to make decisions. Empowering the team and allowing them to work together as well as autonomously is an important "to do." This also builds the team's character. Such delegation is crucial to establishing appropriate team dynamics and decision-making.

The quality of the team and its ability to efficiently and effectively interact with one another is a very important nonfinancial factor. Shared characteristics of high-performing teams include:

- Setting clear, measurable, and prioritized goals that align with the team's purpose.

- Connecting work efforts that "fit" with your organization's mission.

- Ensuring roles and responsibilities are well defined.

- Having high-quality communications.

- Ensuring the team speaks with "one-voice" and reaches effective decisions.

- Creating an environment where commitment, collaboration, innovation, risk-taking, and continuous learning are apparent.

- Ensuring mutual trust, respect, and caring are all built into the team's fabric.

- Putting project and time management tools into practice.

- Celebrating team successes and individual contributions.

Guiding a team to the right decision is a delicate process. To gain their total support of the path that is decided upon, the manager should refrain from stepping in and dictating what to do. More patience is warranted here.

The manager should guide the team to the appropriate decision by asking a series of open- and closed-ended questions through an interactive session. The manager becomes the "facilitator" of the decision-making process, not the decision-maker. If the process is successful, the session will end with the leader receiving the decision they believe is the best outcome based on all mitigating factors and the team embraces the decision. A win-win.

For added flexibility, at set times the team leadership role can rotate, giving others the opportunity to lead and manage the team. This may make even more sense if the team is moving into uncharted waters that require a specific functional skill the current leader is lacking.

Communication is the cornerstone of the team's ultimate success. Establishing an environment whereby members can share differing views and provide constructive criticism without fear of retaliation is crucial. Cohesion and free-flowing knowledge transfer are two additional elements supporting better team dynamics.

As few if any of us work in a utopian environment, the need for barrier removal is important. Such barriers include people conflicts and mistrust, miscommunications and conflicting messaging, and unclear R&R (roles and responsibilities). If these barriers are quickly eliminated, overall team satisfaction and productivity should rise.

> **Lessons Learned**
>
> I was part of a senior team of eighteen to twenty-two members spread globally. Mutual distrust amongst us was an issue. We had very weak meeting agendas that were not driven by the CEO. The same one or two individuals dominated the discussions related to their own agendas. While everyone had a say, rarely were team members who had expertise on various topics asked to share their views. You just had to jump in. We rarely closed out issues efficiently, and these kept reoccurring on our next agenda. Most members did not even know when decisions were reached until we received the post-meeting summary notes. Many of my peers shared these views as well as our staff. During our annual staff alignment and engagement survey, our senior team was routinely viewed as dysfunctional in critical areas of people management, strategy prioritization, and decision-making. This leads me to support much smaller teams led by a more decisive, participative, and engaging personality.

Successful high-performance teams can be described by Aristotle's mantra, "The whole is greater than the sum of its parts," as they usually outperform any one individual's performance.

Strategic Focus

A majority of CEOs state that strategic execution is either the foremost or second most challenging issue they face. I agree. This is not surprising given approximately 87–90% of strategic plans are not implemented

> **Lessons Learned**
>
> During one of my strategic planning processes, we identified over fifty projects being pursued involving hundreds of full-time staff. Less than half of these were in direct support of our new strategic direction. Tough decisions were then made to reduce these and decide which were to continue as our top priorities, including adding some new projects.

successfully. [39] Your focus should only be on what needs to be done, including a clear outline of core activities in sharp detail to secure a competitive advantage. Ignore the rest! Lt. General Robert F. Forman summed it up best when it comes to being focused, when he stated, "If you aim at nothing, you will surely hit it."

Limit the number of strategic priorities, as too many may become overwhelming. For example, to deliver on each strategic objective may require numerous initiatives, building blocks, action items, reporting, tracking, and measurement mechanisms. This can easily and exponentially get out of control. When you must reprioritize existing initiatives or add new priorities, be decisive to reduce or eliminate others to compensate.

Jack Welch once said, "In real life, strategy is actually very straightforward. You pick a general direction and implement it like hell." [6] Steve Jobs once stated, "Simple can be harder than complex: you have to work hard to get your thinking clean to make it simple. [40] But it's worth it in the end because once you get there, you can move mountains." Remember what Socrates said, "Better do a little well, than a great deal badly."

Lessons Learned

Strategic planning is also about what you are "NOT" going to pursue. Such trade-offs are necessary to prevent confusion, frustration, misalignment and wasted resources. Stick to your guns, as many opportunities will continue to arise and could be pursued. But, if they do not align with your strategic intent, say "No thanks."

One last snippet (for now), Peter Drucker is often quoted as saying, "You can't manage what you can't measure." [37] In other words, what you measure is what you get. Establishing two or three KPIs for each strategic objective is enough. Two should be "leading indicators" that forecast the future and one a "lagging indicator" that tracks actual results.

The research of Dyer, et al., [28, 41] indicates there are two alternative strategic viewpoints an organization can pursue: a "process" or "systems" perspective. The process view focuses on people, strategy, and operations. It is a high-level approach that does not go into much detail. Staff may be confused as to how to implement it. The systems view provides much more detail covering–related activities as well as many sub-activities. But on the flip side, a systems view may become overwhelming to implement. It comes down to your own preference and choice.

The systems approach covers topics such as developing the strategy and executing plans, aligning the staff and resources to the best "fit" and continuous tracking, testing, and adapting components. This is my preference if I must choose just one. Maybe a combination of the two viewpoints would work best.

To improve your chances of successful execution, any strategy chosen should include the following steps:

- Strategy definition as to what needs to be achieved and why.
- Alignment of staff and clearly articulating their individual contributions.
- Performance measurement with KPIs (dashboards or a balanced scorecard).
- Continuous progress reports generated to track results.
- Decisive decision-making to keep the plans on schedule.
- Project identification, alignment, and prioritization.
- Continuous communication to clarify team understanding and progress being made.
- Implementation of a reward and recognition plan.

Selecting an appropriate strategy is paramount, as every activity pursued thereafter should support it, or why do it? However, you should expect your strategy to be revised over time due to changing market dynamics. It is a "living" document, not a static one. A few strategic options for consideration, per Michael Porter, [42] that I have implemented include:

Low Cost—Equates to offering low pricing with the goal of gaining market share in narrower market segments. To be successful with this strategy requires a serious effort to take as much cost out of your business as possible to be able to compete with lower prices than your competition. Obviously, your price should not be below your related direct and indirect product costs. Beware, indirect costs are harder to track and allocate accordingly.

Southwest Airlines was a leader at this approach. But sooner or later, most of their competitors were able to lower their cost models and match or beat Southwest's pricing. In today's aviation marketplace, it is a common goal for all airlines to make serious efforts to lower their cost base. Thus, it is no longer unique. Walmart is now in a similar situation within the retail/wholesale market facing stronger competitive "low cost" pricing. I am not a big fan of this approach as a single or dominant strategy as it is a moving target. Plus, everyone is doing it as part of their operations if feasibly possible. Once you achieve lowering your costs, your competitors eventually catch up and you then try to lower your costs again and again to compete. It is an endless cycle, as competing on a lower cost advantage is short-lived and winning on a lower price model does not always bring customer loyalty with it.

Differentiation—Equates to being more competitive and offering unique product features through creating more customer value at a premium price point. Avoid "feature creep" whereby your product manager continues to add new features, and functionality adds to user complexity. These only add to your developmental costs and pricing.

When implemented in large amounts or all at once, users may choose to walk away by selecting a simpler, lower-priced option. Therefore, a phased approach and rollout of new and relevant product enhancements is recommended. Pricing can then be adjusted if warranted. I like this approach as it allows you to uniquely position yourself from others and higher pricing should drive greater profits. Many social media companies are pursuing this approach to stay relevant within their dynamic markets.

Market Segmentation—Equates to taking a broad (horizontal) or narrow (vertical) approach to your market segments. This strategy is a form of diversification and not "putting all your eggs in one basket." Possessing a balanced portfolio of products and services offered within different market segments also balances your risks as well as market opportunities. While some of your segments may be experiencing a downturn, others might be in an upswing. Each counterbalances the other. Numerous consumer goods and cosmetics brands fall under this strategic approach. This is a solid strategy that I have deployed with great successes.

Other possible strategies include:

Value Disciplines—Equates to when the customer's perception is that the distinct value they receive is greater than the price they pay for your service. Focus only on what matters the most to them. This approach aligns with a differentiation strategy. However, the strategic focus is more about creating a strong value proposition. Qatar Airways and Singapore Airlines are very skilled at this approach.

Operational Excellence—Equates to possessing "best in class" processes in any one or numerous business functions and activities (e.g., manufacturing, production, development, sales, logistics, distribution), leading to a unique competitive advantage that is difficult for others to replicate. Walmart and FedEx are two examples of market leaders who perfected their global logistics and distribution models.

This is an extension of a more advanced version of the low-cost model, but you are not required to continually reduce your pricing. Walmart does pass on their lower costs to customers, yet FedEx does not.

Product Leadership—Equates to focusing on de-commoditizing your portfolio of products and services. Product superiority is the main objective. If you are not in a leadership position (#1 or #2 in market share), you should consider divesting. Jack Welch brought this approach to wide acclaim and success at GE. [6] This strategy is a mixture of market segmentation, product differentiation, and value strategies based on how you prefer to position yourself.

Customer Intimacy—Equates to placing the customer relationship at the center of everything you do. The goal is to form a resonant customer relationship measured by loyalty, advocacy, and total customer equity. Every customer touchpoint should be tracked and measured. This is a compelling approach, but only if you make it an organization-wide effort. The retailer, Nordstrom, follows this model, whereby they purposefully have a very high ratio of floor staff to customers. This approach adds to their cost structure. Thus, they have premium pricing, which their loyal customers are willing to pay for such extra attention. Apple and Chick-fil-A are two examples of this approach.

Lessons Learned

In formulating a new growth strategy, the skill sets of our current staff were not aligned with the areas we identified for growth. Therefore, we implemented a restructuring process whereby we reduced overall headcount by 30 percent, while repurposing and adding sixty new positions. The majority of these new positions were in Product Management and Development as well as Sales and Marketing. These changes paid off in a big way.

Whatever strategy you pursue should be aligned with your internal cost structure and brand identity. Ensure you do not chase numerous conflicting strategies, as these will confuse your customers and internal staff.

What are your thoughts?

Does your organization have an RMC (Risk Management Committee)? If not, how might it benefit from RMC creation?

How is your organization addressing the changing multi-generational work environment related to age as well as diversities of gender, ethnicity, race, etc.? How might these efforts be improved and better measured?

Is telecommuting, working from home, and other hybrid work environments successfully practiced within your organization (for which positions and why)?

Have you ever been part of a high-performance team? What characteristics set it apart from other lesser successful teams?

Are your organizations strategic focus and priorities clear and understood by all staff? How may any existing gaps be closed?

Can you articulate your top one to three organizational strategies (e.g., low cost, operational excellence, customer intimacy, etc.)? Do any of these conflict with one another (if so, how)?

CHAPTER 12

Management Decision-Making

Chapter Preview

- **How to better manage the decision-making processes within your professional and personal lives**
- **Why strategic and operational decisions are managed differently**
- **Searching for the optimal decision-making process, structure, and tool.**
- **How to quickly improve the timing, quality, and outcomes of decisions**

Making effective decisions is a critical part of our lives, as we are confronted, daily, with having to make choices. Some decisions are quick and simple, while others take longer and are quite complex. Unfortunately, you may not totally understand the true consequences of your decisions until it is too late, after the fact. Decision outcomes and impacts can make our lives more enjoyable, or can be painful and short-lived or long-term. It is in your hands.

I treat all decisions the same way, giving them the time and attention warranted as even the most trivial ones may have a bigger effect than you might think. Try not to jump too quickly to uninformed conclusions or you may find yourself saying, "Wow, I never thought that would happen." To paraphrase the comedian Chris Rock, who put decision-making into perspective when he stated, "People say life is short. No, it's not. Life is long. And you're gonna have to live with the choices you make for many years to come."

Decision-making is a cognitive process focused on making a choice from other alternatives that results in the selection of a belief or course of action. The goal is obviously to make the "best" decision and receive a positive outcome. To do this well and consistently requires you to give the pending situation your undivided time and attention as well as take certain logical steps to navigate and lessen the magnitude of risk and uncertainty surrounding your eventual decision's outcome.

I utilize the same process and logic for business as well as personal decisions. Some of the following steps may be skipped based on the nature of the decision or its relative importance. The logical steps to make complex business decisions are:

- Avoid stress by allowing to have adequate time to reach your decision.
- Conduct upfront information gathering, quantitative analysis, and research alternatives.
- Weigh all evidence based on pros and cons.
- Align options with your goal to be achieved as well as your personal, corporate policies and values.
- Select the solution and talk it through to rationalize it.
- Decide how to communicate your decision and who needs to know.
- Take decisive action to implement it.
- Review and evaluate the consequences (post-decision).

Managers deal with two main categories of decisions: strategic and operational. The two involve different skill sets for successful implementation. Certain processes, however, can be set up to guide your team through both. A simple guideline to follow is to first frame the discussion by asking a series of questions for your team to debate. This should allow for "brainstorming" to occur as the facts are laid out with a goal of shared understanding. Then, decide what is in scope and out. This prevents your interactions from going off track.

Strategic Decision-Making

Every decision made should align with and support your strategic direction. Otherwise, why on earth would you pursue it? This rationale is the most common way to share why some ideas (while good) should not be undertaken. To lessen frustrations, everyone should understand your shared decision criteria and utilize the framework themselves. Decision criteria I have utilized in the past include:

- **Strategic Fit**—Is this suggested idea within the scope of our strategic direction or not? Does it support our mission and align with our corporate priorities and values?

- **Value Proposition**—Can we establish a unique market position and competitive advantage vs. the competition? Is it compelling, worth pursuing, and wanted or needed by the market?

- **Economic**—Can we make a sustainable profit by pursuing it?

- **Capabilities**—Do we possess the resources to deliver it?

- **Competencies**—Do we have the right expertise and skill sets to successfully execute it?

It should be noted that capabilities and competencies can be acquired through partnerships or outsourcing options.

> **Lessons Learned**
>
> We utilized this decision "checklist" by asking ourselves these questions for every strategic decision to be made. These were meaningful discussions with a lot of learning taking place. Our decisions became more timely, clear, explainable, and relevant.

Lessons Learned

We had numerous success stories while addressing operational decisions. For example, we were able to reduce our annual global production and distribution costs by 2 percent while increasing revenues significantly by implementing the following operational decisions:

- We managed to reduce our inventory levels with decisions related to achieving more efficient forecasting analysis. This led to less inventory being on hand and fewer (less frequent) print runs, lowering setup, and materials costs. This process reduced our obsolete inventories as well.
- We shortened our product development cycles to lower costs and improve our time-to-market deliveries by months. Revenues accrued sooner, improving cashflow.
- We cross-trained our Customer Service team to become a part-time, outbound sales channel (up-selling and cross-selling our services). Eventually, these direct selling efforts occupied 50% of their job time and generated $30 million in revenues as a separate sales channel.
- We implemented a digital "smart" publishing platform and authoring tools that reduced overall production and printing costs by 10–25 percent as we moved to online deliveries.
- We experimented with new models of content delivery such as pricing by "click" (transaction), content licensing, and product bundling with volume discounts.

If we were not able to identify a means to measure the final decision results, they were not pursued.

Operational Decision-Making

Day-to-day, your business should be run in a very agile and nonbureaucratic manner. As you can imagine, hundreds of decisions are made every day at all levels. They are tremendously important as collectively their outcomes have a big impact on your strategic execution. These decisions include product investments, sales, pricing, promotions, managing inventories, logistics, procurement, staffing, and managing customer relationships, just to name a few. There is a direct correlation between your organization's growth and an increase in the number of decisions to be made daily.

As making management decisions can become very complex, Operations Research (OR) tools can be of assistance. OR is a quantitative approach to problem-solving. It uses mathematical modeling techniques to assist decision-makers in times or areas of uncertainty or when differing objectives conflict with one another.

The external business environment can be challenging enough without adding on internal ones. A lack of clear decision rights, architecture, and framework will lead to delays and missed market opportunities, as such market windows close quickly or are captured by competitors.

A golden rule should be, if you hold a colleague accountable for a certain outcome, they must have the authority to drive the related decisions. Misalignment here causes frustrations, delays, and lesser quality decisions.

In certain instances, some decisions should be decentralized while others are better off being centralized. The mix of both will depend on the level of your team's experience and expertise as well as the magnitude and risk of each decision to be reached. For example, while product managers and sales should provide input, pricing and promotional decisions should be centralized within marketing. Product decisions should reside with the product team, with sales and marketing in input. Sales should ultimately decide which distribution channels to pursue for each product with product and marketing input. Related to decentralized activities, local sales teams should be empowered to negotiate agreements within certain pre-determined parameters. Each region should select and recruit their own team members with the Global Head of Sales input. Lastly, the regions should be empowered to identify and select regional venders to partner with relying on the center's functional expertise and advice.

It is also prudent, when possible, to align such decision criteria around Agency Theory. [43] This economic concept involves the relationship between the "principle," who is delegating the work, and the "agent," who performs the work. This theory studies why behaviors and decisions between these two sometimes vary and are contrary, disconnected, or misaligned. The key question to understand is, "Does the agent work in the best interests of the principle or their own?" Setting and aligning the right objectives, goals, incentives, and rewards can address this dilemma. Such alignment should include:

- Shared ownership
- Driving the correct behaviors
- Realistic objectives, but with a stretch incentive
- Shared rewards
- Avoiding conflicting objectives

Lessons Learned

Experimenting with Game Theory [44] is an interesting method to assess and analyze social situations among "rational" individuals within your team using mathematical modeling of their strategic interactions. Participants quickly find that the actions of one directly impact the actions of the other, even though they are acting or reacting independently. The goal of this type of simulation is to optimize decision-making. We tested this in a classroom training environment, with three teams made up of five colleagues and led by an outside instructor. Post-mortem discussions as to why we reached the decisions we made during this simulated exercise were quite interesting.

A decision rights and architecture tool I have successfully used that conceptually maps out and articulates a logical decision methodology is called RAPID (developed by Bain and Co.). [45] These five letters are an acronym that represents the key individuals, and their roles, who need to be engaged in such decisions.

> **Lessons Learned**
>
> Related to Agency Theory, I have witnessed firsthand where conflicting goals and incentives can create frustrations and colleagues working against one another vs. collaboratively. In one instance, our Head of Human Resources had his recruiting budget drastically reduced. The team was being rewarded to not exceed their cost budget. However, our business teams were given aggressive recruiting targets to hire new staff to deliver strong results. This resulted in a "lose-lose" situation that caused much frustration and angst that was the result of poor leadership.

- **R**—The **recommender** of the ultimate decision to be made.

- **A**—The individual who must **agree** with the recommender. There should be just one "R" and one "A."

- **P**—All those who must **perform** or execute the decision. Their input is valuable.

- **I**—All those who are nonperformers, but important in providing **input** to the eventual decision under consideration.

- **D**—The ultimate **decision-maker (decides)**.

For this tool to work seamlessly, the "D" should appoint the "R" and "A" and make these appointments publicly known and clear to everyone. The "R" is chosen based on the ultimate decision truly impacting their business the most. The "A" can be the top SME (subject matter expert) involved. They then solicit input from a number of "Is" and "Ps" to recommend a decision and a way forward. In practice, as the "D," I always told my "R" and "A" that, if they reached a final agreement collaboratively, they would have my approval and could move forward to implementation. This empowerment also assumed they had consulted with all others "Is" and "Ps."

Only if the "R" and "A" could not come to a mutual, final recommendation would I have to step in and make the decision. Trust me, the "R" and "A" always wanted to avoid such a situation of going back to the "D" and saying they were unable to agree. Such failure does not make them look very good as leaders.

The biggest challenge or obstacle I found in successfully implementing the RAPID decision model was when we first put it into practice. We tested RAPID against approximately six to eight unsuccessful pre-RAPID decisions involving many individuals. Ironically, when each person was asked what their letter and role should have been, the vast majority thought they were the "D." Others thought they were an "A," but they were actually an "I." Much of this confusion originated from each individual's egos, people emotions, and control issues. We then knew we had our work cut out for us. Therefore, we rolled out a comprehensive training program on RAPID.

In summary, when you have professional and mature team players, RAPID works well as higher quality decisions are reached in less time while eliminating prior staff frustrations. It also allows those not playing by the rules to be totally visible to everyone.

What are your thoughts?

Can you and your team easily explain your management team's decision-making process and criteria used to reach a quality conclusion (why or why not)?

What criteria is on your own checklist when making strategic decisions?

Within your organization, are those individuals holding the ultimate accountability for results empowered with the authority to make related decisions?

What suggestions would you propose to improve your team's effectiveness to reach quality and timely decisions?

CHAPTER 13

Business Growth Drivers

Chapter Preview

- **Proven low-risk and low-investment approaches (with examples) to spur revenue growth.**

- **Proven moderate-risk and moderate-investment approaches (with examples) to sustain long-term growth through New Product Development (NPDs).**

- **How to expand into new markets through diversification**

- **When and why to pursue partnerships and acquisitions, including critical advice to lessen financial risks**

Organic growth drivers are internally funded, externally focused commercial activities. They involve four key sets of actions that can be deployed to spur topline revenue growth (per Ansoff). [46] These initiatives include market penetration, market development, new product development (NPD), and diversification. Effective implementation of these have a huge impact on your future financial success.

Consideration of potential outside partnerships as well as mergers and acquisitions are alternate options to acquire additional revenues, assets, customer bases, and resources to grow more rapidly than internally driven organic resourcing alone. These will be discussed later.

A more detailed explanation of these four product/market expansion activities for strategic market development is presented below.

Market Penetration

Market penetration involves the upselling and cross-selling of existing services to existing customers in your current markets. Upselling involves adding incremental services to current customer contracts. Examples include adding data coverage or more analytical tools to existing customer contracts. Cross-selling involves offering complimentary services to existing agreements. For example, if a customer is using your publication, you offer them training support or to attend a related conference or some other relevant benefit.

Market penetration is the simplest way to spur growth as you are usually selling additional value to your happiest customers at a very small additional cost and effort on your part. Sometimes, all it takes is a refreshed promotional campaign to build awareness as most customers forget about ads they have seen within a few weeks or a month.

Market Development

This growth driver involves selling existing products and services to new prospects in new market segments. Such market expansion can take many shapes and forms; for example, selling a current data set (where the primary market is airlines) to a secondary market (aircraft manufacturers). Such data could be purchased "as is" or may require some minor modifications or derivatives based on new customer customization requirements. Another example is offering existing airline training courses to other market segments (travel and tourism).

All that is needed for market development is to gain access to and successfully reach out to new prospects while ensuring you understand their respective needs. You will need to build your brand awareness, however, as you are probably not as well known to the new segment as you are with your existing customers.

Both market penetration and market development are mainly sales, marketing, and customer service–related initiatives. They are the least costly growth drivers and can provide numerous "quick win" revenue sources. These initiatives are less expensive to implement as you are either selling additional existing services to happy customers or the same existing services to new prospects. These initiatives can lead to very profitable growth at lower risk thresholds.

New Product Development

New product development (NPD) involves developing and selling new products and services to existing customers. This growth source adds more risk, as it involves some product investments with no guarantee of profitable returns. However, you are selling the new product to current customers and would not create such services unless you already know that demand exists. Plus, mutual trust between you and your customers should already exist as well. Therefore, the risks should be manageable.

In some instances, interested prospects may be willing to share your NPD costs by investing with you to gain an exclusive "first mover advantage" and benefit financially rather than their competitors. This is a great approach to pre-launch and market test your new products or services and gain early, valuable user insights as to "if and how" the new service delivers on its promises. This approach also allows you to fix any identified problem issues with your product or service before moving to a comprehensive global launch.

Lastly, if you are successful in ensuring your pilot users are happy with your new product or service, they can provide valuable testimonials to new prospects. Such third-party "proof" statements are much more credible than anything you can state.

Keep in mind, statistics show that the historical NPD failure rate ranges over 50 percent. This high failure rate is due to the following reasons:

- Pricing options are too numerous and/or complex, confusing prospects.

- Offering different product positioning statements to the same market segment, causing prospect confusion.

- Inability to reach the end user from a sales distribution standpoint.

- Incomplete product (missing key features required by users).

Pricing, promotion, and sales distribution mistakes are the main causes of NPD failures. Ironically, issues with the product itself are less of a problem. Eliminating all these factors through a thorough pre-launch procedure should increase your chances for NPD market success. But missing just one of these can spell disaster.

Successful NPDs are a great method to sustain long-term growth and prosperity. It is crucial that you continue to keep a strong product pipeline of future NPDs. Each NPD in your development pipeline should be tracked in stages. These include:

- An initial market assessment.

- A pilot or alpha test (usually requiring a relatively small investment).

- Building a comprehensive business case to secure the necessary funding to develop the complete product.

- The actual product development.

- The product launch.

- The post-launch evaluation.

It is also wise to monitor how much of your annual revenues is coming from NPDs. Obviously, you want to see this incremental revenue trend increasing year over year; otherwise, growth can easily stagnate. I prefer to see at least 20–30 percent of total revenues derived from NPDs. Achieving this percentage (as a minimum) signals a healthy and sustainable business model. However, this aspirational target takes time to achieve.

To track your percentage of revenues derived from NPDs requires you to define and agree internally with your finance team as to what qualifies as an NPD (define the criteria) and the timeline as to when an NPD matures and is no longer considered "new." We tracked NPD revenues over a maximum two-year period.

> **Lessons Learned**
>
> It is prudent to regularly ask your product development teams the following hypothetical question: "Would you invest your own personal money in this product?" If they say "no," this begs the responding question, "Then, why should we?" You may be surprised as to how many people actually say "no." Not what you want to hear, but sometimes the truth hurts.

Sometimes, an NPD is not 100 percent totally new, but rather an incremental product improvement. We typically defined a product as an NPD when, at a minimum, at least 50 percent of the content was new (with the other percentage coming from an existing product). This allowed us the opportunity to recognize and reward our product team for the creation of NPD derivatives by repackaging existing content. Such derivatives have numerous advantages, as they can usually be produced with a shorter "time to market" window and at a much lower developmental cost.

Launching an NPD requires a collaborative effort beyond your product team. The large investments being made come with an expectation that future revenues will follow, not just covering sunk costs, but generating strong growth and profits.

The sales and marketing teams should be involved in pre-launch and post-launch activities, ensuring projected revenues are aligned and agreed to, with corresponding sales targets. Market analysis and potential prospect input are also important information to gather and share. If this process is not followed and the sales and marketing teams are given a target without their input, frustrations, unhappiness, and a lack of post-launch field sales support are almost guaranteed. The result being an unsuccessful NPD.

Beware of pursing and entering huge markets when you are told by your team "we only need to gain a minimal 5 percent market share to be successful." While the numbers always look good on paper, this 5 percent share of the total market rarely occurs, nor is it always sustainable.

My preference is to support NPDs in markets where there is a plan to establish a "beachhead" in a small niche of a larger market segment. Prove yourself first with a plan to dominate this niche. A goal of gaining no less than a 50 percent market share is not unreasonable. In my view, it is "better to be a big fish in a small pond, than a small fish in a big pond." Once achieved, take a "stepping-stone" approach by expanding into other related niches within the larger market segment. Identify user needs that are aligned and unified vs. trying to address disparate needs between different niche segments.

By following this "stealth" market entry approach, you usually "fly under the radar" and may not be easily detected by the big players (competitors). Thus, they put no pressure on you, allowing all your attention to stay focused on attracting new business vs. defending yourself. Before you know it, success in a few niches can become a larger combined share of the total market than just 5 percent. An appropriate analogy for this is, "You can win many baseball games by hitting singles at the right time. You do not always need to rely on a homerun." The chances of hitting singles are much greater than getting a homerun.

Diversification

> **Lessons Learned**
>
> Identify "quick wins" related to revenue growth that require little to no additional investments. This can be achieved by expanding your sales and marketing spending for existing products utilizing new approaches. Creating derivatives from existing product portfolios is another strategy to accomplish faster growth.

This growth driver involves developing NPDs for new markets. This approach offers the highest level of financial risk as you are moving into lesser or unknown markets and competitive landscapes. You may not totally understand these markets and your brand identity and value proposition may also be unknown to new prospects.

On the other hand, the benefit of diversification is that it offers the greatest growth potential, as you are moving into new and untapped markets. Diversification allows you to expand the size of the markets or the number of markets in which you are competing. The first three growth drivers as discussed above provide the opportunity to gain a larger "piece of the pie" (in your existing market). Diversification allows you to expand the size of the whole pie.

The four organic growth drivers are listed in order of priority for ease of execution, level of risk, and faster returns. I suggest focusing on the first two drivers (market penetration and market development) from the outset, as they require less funding. If rolled out successfully, they will fuel (fund) the latter two initiatives (NPD and diversification) from their profits. Long term sustainability is difficult to achieve without success within these latter two growth categories.

All four of these growth drivers can be achieved internally or by forming strategic partnerships and alliances. The benefits of partnering include speed to access the market and less financial risks. However, the tradeoff with partnerships is that you will be giving up a share of future revenue streams, especially if your partner takes on the upfront development risks. Also, complicated contractual partner agreements could prove difficult to eventually terminate and exit if warranted.

Partnerships

Partnerships usually allow you to penetrate new markets with new solutions in a timely manner and with less financial risk on the front end as these are usually shared between both partners. Partnerships can work in many ways. You can be the dominant market presence that others want to partner with or vice versa.

You can also join a consortium of a few select partners, each adding their own complimentary and unique value. This usually occurs when seeking and bidding on bigger projects where no single organization has the competencies or capabilities to win it on their own. These bids are offered by a "blind" request for proposal RFP (Request for Proposal) process. "Blind" means that you are requested to refrain from making any contact with the RFP originator during the bidding process unless they reach out to you for written clarifications.

Winning such huge bids are nice, but the "spoils" of such triumphs are usually split with your partners by your percentage of contribution. Yet, the risks are not always equally split. Taking on such significant risks requires careful financial considerations as well as purchasing adequate liability and indemnification coverage to protect your organization.

Another point critical to your level of risk tolerance is the location of the jurisdiction where contract disagreements or lawsuits are to be settled. Some countries, such as China and Brazil for example, usually require disputes be settled by their local government and not a neutral third party. Sometimes, this may be negotiated but not very often, based on my own personal experience. If the liabilities they seek are unlimited (which is not that uncommon), we walk away. The prospect of gaining a few million dollars in revenue is not worth the risk of hypothetically losing hundred million dollars in return.

As mentioned, forming partnerships and consortiums has a tradeoff, as you will give away a percentage of future revenues. But if you cannot raise the necessary funding or your organization is averse to assuming such financial risks, partnerships and consortiums are viable options.

If you are a prudent and a creative negotiator, you can financially recognize 100 percent of all revenues on your books (including those of your partner) by securing the following contractual terms, but you must also assume total liability for all customer bad debt:

- You become the "principle" in the relationship.
- Your partner is the "agent."
- You own the intellectual property (IP).
- You are the contracting party with the client.

Achieving these terms will allow you to convert your agent's revenue share into a "cost of sales" (COS) entry on your income statement. This approach is legal and supported by generally accepted accounting principles (GAAP) and International Financial Reporting Standards (IFRS). Stay abreast of these accounting policies, as they can be revised from time to time.

Remember to negotiate your potential exit strategy upfront with your partners. This may not sound appetizing, as it is akin to asking your future spouse for a marriage prenup. But from a business standpoint, this may alleviate future customer pain points or the risk of having either partner at an unfair disadvantage upon termination. By not having negotiated a pre-determined exit strategy, I have experienced both these negative outcomes which were very unpleasant.

Mergers and Acquisitions

Merger-and-acquisition (M&A) activity adds a nonorganic (not internally driven) means to spur topline growth. M&A are pursued for many reasons, such as to:

- Achieve faster revenue growth.
- Quickly add new products and their value proposition to your portfolio.
- Gain new market access and business development expertise.
- Add to your customer base.
- Gain proven IT (information technology) systems and infrastructure.
- Take advantage of potential cost reductions and optimizations through synergies.
- Add new people talent to your team.

However, potential pitfalls include a clash of corporate cultures as well as deep resistance and animosity between the organizations. There is more to focus on beyond strategic fit. If the two merging teams are fierce competitors, they might not like one another much. Other pitfalls may include IT/infrastructure mismatches, unforeseen legal liability and indemnity risks, and the possible defection of key talent on both sides.

The acquirer should not "give away the fort" (pay too much) during negotiations in the way of concessions or the acquiree may end up calling the shots in future. Nor should the acquirer "stack the deck" after the acquisition with their team assuming all the leadership roles. Being too timid during the integration phase will cause you to continuously make painful and distracting changes post acquisition. Try your best not to overpay by being aware of the "hockey stick" growth curve proposed by the acquiree, as it rarely comes to fruition. This scenario is when the acquiree has previously delivered a historical trend of slow or modest growth. But, in its outer forecast years, it projects a huge growth curve to justify a larger valuation multiple affecting its price tag. Do not be fooled by such suspect sales pitches.

To avoid negative M&A surprises, a comprehensive due diligence process needs to be undertaken prior to closing any deal. This comprehensive process will take many months to conclude based on the acquiree's size, scope, and complexities. Uncovering and addressing areas of concern can also support your final negotiation position.

The due diligence process requires both parties to execute a non-disclosure agreement (NDA). These agreements, while usually relatively short compared to the final contract, can include tricky "legalese" language as well. I have witnessed on numerous occasions the acquiree requesting that if no deal is completed, the acquirer agrees to not compete in the acquiree's markets for a certain number of years. These are usually markets you are already competing in or plan to enter with or without the acquiree. Do not give up your rights!

If you can get beyond the NDA, areas to further investigate and review include, but are not limited to:
Market segments being served

- Customer bases
- Current and pending commercial agreements
- Organizational structure alignment and fit
- Staffing (people talent)
- Compensation practices
- Commercial operations and practices

- Intellectual property rights and patents
- A detailed legal and financial review/audit covering all related financial reporting and tax documentation

Your due diligence team should consist of experts with the functional expertise needed. If you do not possess all these experts internally or your team cannot be taken away from their day jobs and responsibilities for a long period of time, going outside for such assistance is another option for consideration.

A tried and tested method to reduce the risks of M&A activities is to first partner with the potential candidate. This allows you to get to know them better and work with them on the front end before bigger financial commitments are made. If you both eventually like what you see, taking the relationship to the next level can then be pursued.

> **Lessons Learned**
>
> When executing a M&A agreement, always ensure you protect your own organization by securing noncompete agreements with key management personnel and functional experts of the acquiree who decide to take their money and run. I suggest a term of no less than ten years if they will agree. I have witnessed a lesser timeline backfire as we ended up competing again with the same people we paid to acquire. In reality, you can end up funding your own competition.

Value Creation

When it comes to driving future growth, a related component to keep in mind includes value creation. This premise is based on the concept of giving something of value to receive something of more value in return. To receive value, you normally must give it.

Value can be built or destroyed. If the benefits of your product or service are perceived by the prospect as something they need and are greater than the price they pay, value is created even if it is emotional. How will the prospect's life be better based on the benefits they gain? If value is not visualized and understood, the prospect will rarely purchase. Value creation is not just for external purposes as it can occur inside your organization as well. In summary, as Carmine Gallo, an author, coach, and keynote speaker, stated, "Sell dreams, not products." [27]

Quality

Quality is another component to consider related to driving growth. Quality is a standard measured against other similar things. It is a degree of excellence, superiority, or worth. Quality can be a noticeable judgment of how excellent something is or how well something is made. The opposite is also true.

Lessons Learned

When a product fails in a market, it is not uncommon to have internal finger-pointing related to whose fault it was. The production team blames the sales team for a lack of effort, while the sales team blames the production team for delivering a product that does not meet the market's needs. Which scenario is correct?

A post-mortem product launch meeting should be held between both teams (and others that are close to the situation) to truly understand the facts and reasons behind the lack of success. Even if the issues cannot be resolved, the flaws will at least be well documented and hopefully prevent the possibility of reoccurring.

I recommend conducting such P&S post mortem meeting for successful launches as well. The goal is to learn what led to your success with the idea to replicate these within other P&S's still to be launched.

Quality can be achieved externally with customers and internally with operational improvements within your organization. Such internal improvements can be measured and take the shape of cost controls, on-time performance, lowering failure rates, or defective frequencies. Customer quality attributes include accessibility, accountability, accuracy, reliability, affordability, and trustworthiness.

If you care about quality, one way to improve your chances of success is to implement a Quality Management and Assurance Program to oversee all related processes and activities to accomplish and maintain a desired level of excellence. Having such a program in place can add credence and proof of quality in the minds of your customers.

> **Lessons Learned**
>
> Quality is validated by the customer, not internally by your product teams. Otherwise, how can a product that is held in the highest esteem by your internal team fail miserably in the marketplace? I say this from experience.

What are your thoughts?

Is NPD (new product development) a priority within your organization?

Is your new product developmental pipeline effectively monitored and frequently communicated?

Is a clear NPD process (and its logical steps) in place and followed?

Do you know your organization's overall market success rate (e.g., percentage for NPD launches)? Are your market failures discussed and lessons learned shared?

Is your organization geographically diversified within multiple market segments? Do future expansion opportunities exist (where, why, and how)?

What steps can be put in place to ensure any new strategic partnerships do not fail?

Is your organization's value proposition and benefits clear to your customer base? How can these be enhanced and better articulated?

Is Quality a priority for your organization? How is it measured?

CHAPTER 14

Financial Management

Chapter Preview

- Key financial terms and principles you "need to know" that can significantly impact business results.

- Key financial information and decisions resulting from analysis of the Income Statement, Balance Sheet, and Cashflow Statements.

- Additional financial activities that can increase revenues, fund business operations, and ensure long term sustainability.

- How effectively managing your sales pipeline can improve short-term revenues and more accurately forecast future long term revenue streams

This chapter covers the function of finance. This discipline is the foundation of a business as it involves the planning and decision-making around the purchase of assets, goods, raw materials, and other related resources to meet the needs of an organization. Finance is the lifeblood of your organization, as it is virtually impossible to function without it. It ensures the adequate flow of funds to operate your organization by being concerned with profitability, costs, cash, credit, etc., as the means to achieve your business objectives.

Key financial terms and principles you should be familiar with and better understand include:

- **Time Value of Money (TVM)**—Also referred to as Present Discounted Value, TVM recognizes the relative worth of future cashflows which are generally lower than current cashflows due to inflation. TVM also considers the opportunity costs of the funds being held. This principle explains that there is a greater benefit of receiving money now (in the present) than receiving the identical sum later, as it can be invested now and can generate incremental cashflow. An example of this would be depositing this money into a bank account where the depositor would receive interest income.

- **Return on Investment (or Cost)**—A formula to determine an investments profitability. It is calculated by taking your Net Income divided by your total costs. Multiplying this amount by 100, converts into a percentage.

- **Payback Period**—It is the length of time (in months or years) for an investment to recover its initial funds outlay.

- **Cashflow**—Tracking and understanding the movement of money (cash) in or out of a business over a given period is critical to manage. Such cashflows result from operating, financing, and investing activities. Common metrics used by organizations to measure cash include: Net Present Value (NPV), used to value a business; Internal Rate of Return (IRR), used to determine the rate an investor will receive; and Cash Conversion Ratio, which is the amount of time from payments you make for items such as Cost of Goods Sold (COGS) to when you receive a payment from a customer.

- **Capital Structure**—This is the foundation of business finance. It shows how an organization is financing itself to gain money or capital. These funds come through various sources, usually a combination of equity and long-term debt.

- **Expense Management**—Expense management tracks employees' spending activities and their reimbursement through an expense reconciliation and reporting tool.
- **Budgeting**—Budgeting is the tactical implementation of the business plan. Budgets deploy numerous control measures to track results. Budget categories that are typically tracked include operations, capital, and cash.
- **Liquidity**—This concept details how well an organization can meet its short-term financial obligations. If it cannot do so, additional debt will need to be incurred. The trick is to collect monies owed to you faster than you pay others. While such practices may seem unfair to your vendors and suppliers, it is very common in business. Trust me, they are all trying to do the same to you. However, try not to hurt your smaller vendors who need to make their bi-weekly payroll and pay their own suppliers.
- **Risk/Return Tradeoffs**—This concept compares the potential amount of reward on a particular investment relative to the comparable risk undertaken with the investment. Its premise states that low risks should equate to low returns, while higher risks equate to higher returns. This is obviously a speculative premise with no guarantees unless a fixed rate of return is locked in.

There are three primary financial statements that are commonly used to report and track the financial activities and performance of your organization. These are the Income Statement, Balance Sheet, and Cashflow Statement. It is imperative that these are all used in unison. Due to their importance, let's review them in more detail, as each brings a unique perspective to your ever-changing financial position.

Income Statement

This report is also referred to as the Profit and Loss Statement (P&L). It reports Net Income over a specific time period. Net Income is calculated as your total earned revenues minus total expenses. It translates Net Revenues into Net Earnings as either a profit or loss. Your P&L is presented in a standard format that shows revenues, expenses, gains, or losses and (Net Income) in this exact ordering.

Revenues—Revenues are at the heart of the P&L. Without revenues, you have no P&L, no potential profit or thriving business. Establishing multi-year, reoccurring revenue streams, where possible, is an ideal business model. This business practice, based on specific product and service delivery methods to the customer, allows you to carry over a percentage of these reoccurring revenues from your current fiscal year into the following year.

The benefit this practice presents is that your organization can project and recognize such future revenues in your next fiscal year's P&L. Otherwise, your revenue base next year needs to be grown from scratch. Some products and services can possess a reoccurring revenue stream carryover of at least 80 percent. Certain data services based on multi-year contracts offer this huge benefit. Generally Accepted Accounting Principles (GAAP) dictates such carryover rules and the method for doing so.

Possessing a healthy sales pipeline and tracking newly closed deals is the best indicator to project future revenue streams. Qualified

> **Lessons Learned**
>
> Not understanding the accounting reporting guidelines of revenue recognition can be very detrimental to your P&L and organization's overall financial position. Mistakes can be very costly to your bottom line and variances can seriously impact financial forecasting. You also run the risk of an external financial audit and could face possible fines.

sales leads or potential prospects are known as your qualified pipeline (QP). Your QP should be categorized, tracked, updated, and discussed on a frequent basis.

> **Lessons Learned**
>
> Additional incremental revenues, such as securing product upgrades at a higher price point with existing customers, should be tracked. Due to the sheer number of these, my organizations only tracked those in excess of $100,000. But the values being tracked will vary from business to business. These are "low hanging fruit" to be seized.

The goal of such discussions is to implement creative tactics to shorten the sales cycle and bring in these new revenues as quickly as possible. Such incentives to purchase earlier may include discounts offered to close the agreement by a specific date, volume discounts, and adding a complimentary service component to the package. These are all positive rewards. However, the opposite approach may sometimes be necessary and include such tactics as stating the negotiated price is only valid until a certain date, after which the original, higher list price will be enforced. As you can imagine, this "threatening" approach can impact your goodwill, as your credibility can be damaged. While you can come across as desperate, this approach is sometimes necessary when prospects keep delaying the purchase.

QP categories or stages to track during the selling cycle include:

- Prospects that show initial interest in your solution.
- When a proposal is sent to them.
- When official negotiations have begun.
- When an agreement is executed, the product is delivered, and revenues are recognized.

Successful agreement closures, including the total contract length and dollar value associated with each closure, can then be calculated to forecast future revenue streams.

Leaving potential prospects in your QP that have been tracked for many years can skew or mislead and overestimate your true QP value. On the other hand, I have witnessed "floundering" deals being secured and finally closed after five to ten years! Many times, this is due to a revolving door (continuous turnover) in the prospect's upper management team or a consensus decision-making model whereby everyone on their management team must sign off on the agreement, even if they have no interest in it or use for the product or service. Thus, it is your call to establish tracking guidelines to determine whether long-lingering deals are truly moving forward. Avoid allowing a small percentage (of the total value) of lingering deal to be reported in your QP as this exact amount will never occur. It will logically be the full deal value or nothing. Your QP accuracy is critical.

Lessons Learned

My experience tells me that you need a QP dollar value of at least two to three times larger than your sales target. This ratio can vary based on your sales team's historical track record and past success rates of closing new or incremental contracts. The sales cycle is also key here as it traces how long it takes to close a given deal. As stated, this timeline can span a few weeks, months, or even years!

Keep in mind, the dollar value of sales contracts may not always equate to the dollar amount of revenues you can recognize in any given year. This is due to varying revenue recognition models per product and service type as well as how and when each are delivered (e.g., licensing, subscriptions, data dumps, consulting). Not to mention, many sales contracts span over multiple years. Thus, having a solid understanding of GAAP and IFRS policies is paramount to avoid unnecessary financial surprises when recognizing and reporting current and future revenue streams.

Expenses—These activities, otherwise known as costs, are customarily matched and tracked against their corresponding revenues within your P&L. This matching process can be carried out by an accounting method called "Activity-Based Costing" or (ABC), perfected by Robin Cooper. [47] This managerial accounting practice is based on the inclusion of all direct and indirect activities related to a product or service. Each activity is assigned a cost according to actual consumption. This method provides a better view of the "true costs" vs. the more arbitrary conventional costing methods. Benefits from using the ABC method are that it allows you to implement a more viable pricing strategy and calculate more accurate profitability.

There are three main types of expenses to be tracked: Operating expenses are those needed to run your daily business activities (e.g., administration, salaries, taxes, lease fees, etc.). These are sometimes called fixed expenses. The second cost type is variable expenses, such as COGS and sales commissions, which vary based on increases or decreases in sales volumes or production levels. Some expenses may be categorized as "prepaid," which are future expenses paid in advance. This approach is not always a prudent tactic as it effects your current cashflow position.

> **Lessons Learned**
>
> If you do not have a healthy bottom-line profit, you may need to seek loans as a funding alternative. This approach can prove very costly, risky and may result in your organization becoming financially beholden to outside financial institutions or private equity firms. Your organization can easily lose its financial freedom.

These are recorded as expenses in your Income Statement. The third type are Capital Expenses (CAPEX). These are incurred expenses for future benefit. Examples are fixed assets (facilities, equipment, intangible assets such as patents, etc.). These investments in your business are considered assets and recorded within your Balance Sheet. As a reminder, these CAPEX assets amortization and depreciation are recorded as expenses within your Income Statement. Do not be caught off guard and remember to track these as they can be significant amounts.

Profits—Profitability is your ability to earn more revenues than expenses. Key indicators related to your profit include Net Sales (or Gross Margin), which is Revenues minus COGS; Profit Margin, which is Net Income divided by Net Sales; and Gross Profit (%), which is calculated as Gross Margin divided by Net Sales.

Balance Sheet

The balance sheet is a presentation of the organization's assets, liabilities, and shareholder equity positions at a given point in time. It is primarily used for computing your rate of return and evaluating your capital structure. It gives a "static" financial snapshot of what your organization owns and owes as well as amounts invested by shareholders.

Its basic formula is: Assets = Liabilities + Shareholder Equity. The balance sheet's premise is that your organization must pay for what it owns (its assets) by borrowing money (thus taking on liabilities) and/or taking money from investors (and issuing shareholder equity).

> **Lessons Learned**
>
> I cannot overemphasize the importance of negotiating the terms of your receivables (money owed to you) to be collected within a shorter time period. They should usually be payable within thirty days without penalties. While your payables (money you owe others) should have payment terms of up to ninety to 120 days. In this scenario, you will have an up to a ninety-day "float" on your monies received. By the way, poor cashflow generation (having insufficient cash on hand) is a leading cause of the failures of many small businesses.

Assets—Presented in their order of liquidity (ease of converting into cash), assets come in two categories:

- **Short-Term Assets**—Cash, accounts receivable, inventories, prepaid expenses, and "working capital" used in day-to-day operations (e.g., raw materials, salaries, wages, rent, and taxes).

- **Long-Term or "Fixed" Assets**—Where liquidity is longer than twelve months out. Land, buildings, equipment, and intangible assets such as Intellectual Property (IP), goodwill (also known as Brand Equity) fall within this group of assets.

Liabilities—These include monies owed from your bills and invoices as well as loans from financial institutions. The two main categories are:

- **Current Liabilities**—Due in less than twelve months (e.g., bank debt, interest due, wages, and accounts payable)

- **Long-Term Liabilities**—Due beyond twelve months (e.g., longer term debt, deferred taxes)

Shareholder Equity—This is the money attributed to your shareholders. Your organization's "Net Worth" is calculated as Total Assets minus Total Liabilities. Retained Earnings (or Net Earnings) are also important, as they can be a cash-based source of funds to invest in business operations, pay off debt, or distribute as dividends to shareholders.

A key financial ratio to evaluate your amount of financial leverage is "debt-to-equity." It is calculated by dividing Total Liabilities by Shareholder Equity. It shows your degree of financing through debt vs. through wholly owned funds. The higher this ratio, the greater its risk to shareholders. As a side note, this ratio is also important to review before you invest your own hard-earned cash in other companies (stock market).

The balance sheet does have some limitations though. It is a "static" view at a single point in time to compare your financial health to other historical periods. It can also be misleading relative to how you amortize and write off your depreciation of such things as IT investments, buildings, and other infrastructure investments. These long-term write-offs directly and negatively impact your P&L, as they are reported as an annual expense hurting your profit position. Planning and forecasting for this annual occurrence is very important.

> **Lessons Learned**
>
> As a prudent manager, you should continually ask yourself and others the ultimate question: "Do we have enough cash and short-term assets to cover our financial obligations?"

Lastly, balance sheet transactions are usually accrued and recognized once an economic event or business transaction occurs (not when the money is exchanged). This is different from how such transactions are recorded on your Cashflow Statement (see below). Confusion may easily occur between these two important financial statements, which will end in obvious financial pain if not managed properly.

Cashflow Statement

This financial report encompasses the following sections:

- **Cash inflows** from all business operations and **cash outflows** that pay for these business activities.

- **Financing activities**, which are cash inflows and outflows from debt and equity.

- **Investment activities** (gains and losses) over a specific time.

The sum of these three activities is termed "Net Cashflow." Within the cashflow statement, cash is recognized "ONLY" when payment occurs and is received, which is different from how it is recorded on the balance sheet, as previously stated.

There are other important financially related activities effective managers can undertake that also affect these three financial statements. If implemented effectively, they can produce positive results. If neglected, the financial outcomes are opposite. Let's review a few of these to better understand how they may improve your overall financial position and what you can do to ensure this occurs.

Additional Financial Activities

Bad Debt—Bad Debt (BD) are debts from a revenue source that cannot be recovered. BD terms may vary, but once a receivable is past due (beyond its normal payment terms), it becomes an expense and negatively impacts your Income Statement until the time it is recovered (in part or in full).

Lessons Learned

Collecting BDs can be a tricky practice. When larger amounts were due to us from big customers, we always involved the product manager and/or local salesperson in the customer interactions. We never left these accounts to the sole discretion of the BD collector. In many instances, these customers were considering additional purchases and we did not want to upset them with blind threats from someone not close enough to their situation or payment history. This is a "fine line" to walk as some large customers notoriously and consistently pay late, but do eventually pay.

Why does this occur? Because the customer knows they have the "clout" based on their power position and financial obligations owed to you. They are effectively managing their cashflows as well. Getting these payments late is better than not getting them at all. When this situation occurs, and it will, you just have to "bite the bullet" and take a related hit to your own cashflow.

If the BD is not recoverable, you will lose any interest penalties tied to this debt as well. If the BD is eventually collected, an accounting reversal is made as the BD expense no longer exists. This BD expense becomes recovered revenues, which is a good thing to occur and generally worth the effort and expense put forth to collect them.

Budgeting—The practice of budgeting represents the tactical implementation of your business plan (financial road map), including performance measurement. The first question it addresses is, "How do you plan to beat last year's performance?" The budget is really your operating plan. It addresses what funds are needed to successfully deliver your business plans (i.e., operational, capital, and cashflow). The budget also allows you to forecast against it. The business cycle or timeline for such financial projections will vary depending upon your organization's financial policies; however, the more frequent you forecast against your budget, the better.

The budgeting process usually begins approximately six months before the start of your next fiscal year. Corporate financial calendars vary as to when they start and are completed.

Costs (expenses) should be matched and follow revenues from a reporting standpoint. This is important because, if these two are not phased appropriately, cashflow can be negatively impacted. Remember, "cash is king."

> **Lessons Learned**
>
> Setting up an internal or outsourced BD collection service is highly recommended. Because even when the customer's invoice is past due, if they verbally agree to pay, you can recognize their revenue immediately. But not without some associated risk, of course, and it is always better to secure any customer commitments in writing. Making a concerted effort to collect BD can generate millions of dollars back to your organization. Remember, these were for services you had already expensed, rendered, yet considered them lost. These collections go straight to your bottom line (profits).

> **Lessons Learned**
>
> Create an internal "fiscally responsible" work environment where colleagues spend company funds as if they were spending their own family's money.

> **Lessons Learned**
>
> Related to spending on marketing activities, if you cannot track and measure the ROI, pass on it. Many social media and other useful analytical marketing tools exist to support such ROI monitoring.

Specialized training should be a requirement for everyone involved in budgeting as budget mistakes are usually very costly and result in unexpectedly missing your financial results, targets, and related financial incentive rewards. I am a big supporter of "zero-based" budgeting. This approach requires you to build your next year's budget from scratch, not based on what you spent the prior year. This practice should also prevent your team from irresponsibly trying to unnecessarily spend all their remaining budget left before the current year ends. They fear if they do not spend it, they might lose it next year. Yes, this behavior does occur. Building your budget from scratch prevents such expense spending comparisons as you only request what you need as each year has its own set of unique spending requirements.

New Projects—A new project is typically a "one-off" initiative that usually does not regularly reoccur. In most instances, they are expensed through special funding "below the line" outside your operation's P&L. Once a project is completed and you decide to go forward with it, the project is then moved into your normal operational plans and tracked as part of your ongoing operations. If such projects negatively affect your financial operating position, discontinuing some of these might be considered.

Capital Investments—As mentioned earlier, capital investments or capital expenditures (CAPEX) are usually longer term (multi-year) and larger investments in fixed assets (e.g., IT, infrastructure, facilities) that are tracked and written off from your balance sheet to your P&L. As stated earlier, their depreciation cost eventually hits your P&L as an expense on an annual basis. Investing wisely here bring your business strategic and operational benefits based on their type.

Funding for CAPEX can come from multiple sources, either secured through loans or through a promise to repay in a future lump sum by shareholder equity and/or retained earnings (cash). Longer-term loans are riskiest due to varying interest rates on such loans. A key indicator to track here is that your ROI is greater than the interest rate on your related debt.

Creating a customized scorecard (a set of KPIs) that allows you to monitor your key financial indicators on a daily, weekly, monthly, and quarterly timeline is prudent. Such scorecards are historically based (after the fact) and can be useful for conducting trend analysis. These are not, however, a replacement for forecasting future results but are a means to do so.

Lessons Learned

Deciding how and where to fund new projects bring interesting challenges. When new projects are proposed, I have found that the requirement for new full-time equivalent (FTE) staff can usually be filled by repurposing existing resources, not requiring additional staff.

Challenge your colleagues who are seeking funds for new projects to identify which current projects can be stopped or reduced to fund and staff their new projects. If your colleagues are honest, transparent, and fair, usually enough existing funds and FTEs can be freed up elsewhere for these new initiatives.

What are your thoughts?

What key financial metrics does your organization track and report? What additional KPIs can better assist you?

Does your organization create an individual Income Statement for each P&S? What benefits would such provide?

Does your organization have an efficient BD (bad debt) collection process? Do you know your average annual BD collection rate?

Does your organization actively communicate new sales to staff? Is a "sales prospect" pipeline tracking mechanism utilized to forecast future revenue streams?

CHAPTER 15

Managing the Four Ps

Chapter Preview

- Key strategies, techniques, and tools to successfully manage a P&S portfolio.

- How to rejuvenate a product in decline

- Complexities of pricing, and where to focus attention and efforts.

- Promotional techniques to increase sales and track ROI.

- How to maximize returns from all sales/distribution channels

Lessons Learned

Knowing where each of your products stand within their own lifecycle phase, allows you to better manage the other related Pricing, Promotion and Place decisions (see below).

The four Ps of the marketing mix are Product, Price, Promotion, and Place. [48]

1. Product

Every commercial organization goal is to offer some form of product or service of value. Product management centers on portfolio management through product updates, enhancements and creating new products and services while managing the lifecycle (e.g., introduction, growth, maturity, and decline) of each product or service.

The Boston Consulting Group (BCG) Growth-Share matrix [49] offers one viable method to categorize and manage your product portfolio into four buckets:

- **Stars**—Exhibiting strong, profitable growth.
- **Question Marks**—With potential upside, but unproven.
- **Cash Cows**—Experiencing market saturation with strong revenues but flat growth.
- **Dogs**—Needing to be discontinued.

A product strategy I like to utilize is to build end-to-end, integrated solutions focused beyond the primary product offering, which involves unique (add-on) service components. This should prevent the need for your customers to go elsewhere for additional support beyond what you are currently offering them.

If possible, ensure customer switching costs (the cost and effort required for a customer to shift to a competitor) are very high. The goal is to offer greater quality, value, uniqueness, and post-sales support at a fair price. Creating such loyalty will lock your customers in for the long term. Such an approach may also keep away new competitors, as the barriers of market entry may be perceived as too steep and costly to pursue. Tactics to achieve this enviable market position include:

- Executing long-term customer contracts.
- Offering steep pricing discounts offset by significant customer penalties for early termination.
- Integrating your service as a critical component embedded within your customers operations. Changing your service requires changing the customers operational procedures.
- Creating value-added customized reporting tools that cannot be easily replicated.

- Embedding your service into other vender offerings used by the customer. Changing from yours requires the customer to also change away from the other vender.

Ultimately the goal is to have your customer realize for themselves that the time, effort, and cost of switching from your proven service is not worth the perceived benefits of a competitor's promises.

As briefly mentioned earlier, avoid "feature creep" when rolling out new products or services. If you plan to add new features and functionalities, do so in stages or phases (e.g., release one, release two, and so on) and not all at once. The point here is to avoid overengineering, which adds costs and unnecessary user complexity all at once. The higher the number of features, the higher the cost to produce, which usually ends in a higher price point. If you are not careful, this "overbuild" can push prospects to lower priced, simpler alternatives, as many of your features may not be of use or a priority for them. Once you learn this lesson the hard way, then trying to adjust your price lower after such large investments will not only kill your profit margins, but may eventually end up killing the service as well.

It is important to know how and when to kill or phase out unprofitable products and services. This sounds logical, but it is not always put into practice, as it is easier to "let sleeping dogs lie." The same can be said for NPDs that are floundering in development, showing little perceived market potential. It is commonplace for underperforming products or services to stay alive as these may be the primary roles of certain staff. They sometimes believe if the product or investment goes away, their job may as well. From their perspective, this rationale makes complete sense.

The solution should be to stop these unprofitable products and unwise investments and then try your best to find these colleagues other work within your organization. Such a practice not only reinforces your loyalty to those being transitioned, it reassures the rest of your staff that you act in a fiscally responsible way, but with empathy and fairness. By doing the right thing, their comfort level takes a positive jump as well. It makes little financial sense to continue to throw good money after bad. Just pull the plug and reinvest these funds in more opportunistic areas.

As I stated in the preceding section on financial management, all related costs (direct and indirect) should follow the revenues of each product. If this accounting practice is not followed, you will never have an accurate view of each product's individual profit margins. Without such a view, you may continue to invest where funds are not justified or warranted.

Lessons Learned

Many Product Managers (PMs) tend to focus on their existing products and enhance those, while neglecting NPD efforts, as these are not easy to accomplish and brings significantly more financial risk. Their rationale (excuse) is always the same, they do not have the time and will need someone else to do this for them. A poor excuse, so do not accept it.

This behavior can be easily and quickly addressed by agreeing upon and setting NPD development and revenue targets for each PM. In my organizations, I went to the lengths of agreeing upon how much of the PM's future efforts should be spent on new product development. I say no less than 25 percent. These new efforts and expected outcomes become a prioritized PA objective that will dictate their future success, or lack thereof, as a PM.

Lessons Learned

It is possible to rejuvenate a product or service by reversing its course to an earlier stage within its lifecycle. Our biggest selling product, which had been in the market for fifty years, had not been growing for as long as we could remember. It was a "fat" and valuable Cash Cow for us. While it had a huge following of loyal users, we were not able to attract new, younger customers as they perceived it as old, tired, and dusty. The product's delivery cycle of content updates and feature enhancements was historically set for revision every three years. Our competitors did the same. This industry practice seemed to be written in stone and everyone, including all customers, accepted and abided by this unwritten rule. Who would dare to rock the boat? We did!

First, we conducted extensive research (by market segment) to identify what exactly this younger generation of potential customers wanted and needed. We then built our revised product exactly to these new specifications, while ensuring we did not alienate our current user base as well. We simultaneously created and launched a promotional campaign directed specifically to each prospect's exact interests, as we knew who they were. Lastly, we broke the traditional three-year product delivery cycle by drastically shortening our developmental efforts. We launched our significantly revised product one year earlier. This sneak attack caught all our competitors by surprise and flatfooted with our latest content and new features.

Needless to say, we took the market by storm as our competition had very little to offer the market in response. Our existing and new customers were thrilled while our competitors were not. This product went from being at the end of its maturity with flat sales to back into the growth stage. A huge success story.

2. Price

This "P" can prove to be one of the most difficult to successfully implement as there are many strategies and related decisions that come into play. Some of these issues that warrant serious discussion include:

- Pricing models—Premium, low cost, cost plus, loss leader?

- Pricing strategies—Increase profit margins, gain market share, penetrate new markets?

- Lifecycle—Which phase is the product or service in?

- Volume and list price discounting policies?

- Number of competitors and their varying pricing models?

- Multiple currencies and fluctuation impacts—Your revenues may be collected in one currency, while your product costs may be expensed in another or even multiple currencies. These need to be closely tracked as the relative value of your revenues may go down while your costs go up. Where is the best location (cost-wise) to produce your product and what local currencies you are willing to accept for payment?

Regarding price discounts, I suggest setting a proposed list price that covers your costs and allows some flexibility for discounting as almost everyone wants to negotiate. If your list price is set realistically and your proposed discount range is acceptable to the customer, your resulting product profitability should be easier to ascertain. Set these percentage discount ranges upfront, which allows your local sales team to confidently negotiate within these parameters, not having to continually involve product management.

If a prospect states that your price is too high, your team may not have explained its true value correctly. If they have done so correctly, the value is obviously not justifiable to the prospect. Walking away at this point is better than discounting more, as you will just kill your margins and rarely build customer loyalty.

Always stay close to what your competitors are charging as a benchmark or reality check. But avoid matching crazy price discounts of desperate competitors trying to throw their own organization a final lifeline. If you do foolishly match them, they might react by going even lower as they have little to lose. This is a short-term game, as they will soon go away and then you are stuck with much lower prices and margins. This is a lose-lose scenario. Eventually increasing your prices again will usually require you to justify them by adding additional value. Therefore, avoid this game at all costs.

Lessons Learned

At one of my prior organizations, we produced a product that was the market leader. Customers told us frequently that they used it because it was the "best" and "highest quality" product on the market. Their loyalty was amazing.

Based on these customer perceptions, I requested our team conduct a quick competitive pricing analysis. We learned our product was priced in line with our second and even third-level competitors. I then challenged our product and marketing teams that our product deserved a premium price, well above the competition. They did not agree, stating that if we did so, we would lose market share. Such a pricing assumption is difficult to validate with your customers, as very few will ever admit to you that your price is too low.

I eventually won this internal debate by taking full responsibility if I was wrong. With our fingers crossed, we increased the price, lost no customers and instantly added three million dollars to our bottom line (profits).

Lessons Learned

At one of my organizations, we produced over 300 publications. All were priced exactly the same, which made little sense. Their page counts, sizes, production costs, and market value were completely different.

One of our Marketing Managers (MM) sent out an automatic renewal notice on one of our many publications. Based on the renewal notice, if the customers did not respond and decline our renewal within thirty days, they were automatically invoiced.

Once sent, the MM noticed a mistake was made and the price on the invoice was double that was set in the prior year. The MM wanted to send out a corrected invoice. I took this opportunity as a teaching moment and challenged our pricing philosophy of having identical pricing for all publications. I wanted to prove my point that having a "one price fits all" model was fiscally irresponsible. So, I said, "Let's test this concept in practice and see what impact this huge price increase has on our traditional renewal rate of this publication." The MM reluctantly agreed.

When the dust settled and all renewals were in, the good news was that our renewal rate actually jumped 5 percent vs. the prior year. The bad news was that I found out for sure that we knew little about how to price.

Lessons Learned

Another bad pricing story... We once launched an app with many content-delivery options and functions to choose from, each with its own pricing. We subsequently promoted approximately ten different pricing models (one for each option). This created mass confusion, both internally and externally, and led to the quick demise of this service. I did challenge my team before our launch as to why we needed so many complex pricing options, but I did not stop them. My mistake!

The following are some general guidelines for pricing strategies and variances at various stages of the product lifecycle. These are just guidelines, as there are always exceptions.

- **Introductory Stage**—Decrease prices to gain market share and recover sunk costs.
- **Growth Stage**—As market demand grows, increase prices, as new features and value should continue to be added based on user requirements.
- **Maturity Stage**—Hold prices stable or even decrease prices a little to try to hold on to market share if stronger competition exists.
- **Declining Stage**—Increase prices as you will want to "milk" the product for revenues until your "die hard" customers eventually shift away. This pricing strategy is also useful to apply when you want to shift customers to a newly upgraded product (e.g., to digital or online content from a traditional printed version). In this example, the traditional product's price should be much higher than the digital version. This helps persuade your customer base to shift over. The rationale being that print publications costs increase (per unit) as print volumes decrease. Online content delivery costs are not normally affected by volume swings.

3. **Promotion**

The key objective of your promotional activities is to increase sales. Other benefits include:

- Creating product or brand awareness.
- Identifying new prospects.
- Securing product trials.
- Providing specific product details.

- Educating users.
- Building brand equity.

Actions to consider when creating a promotional campaign are numerous but starts with defining your target audience. You want the prospect to take some type of action. Referring them to your website or customer service center is a good option. Utilize multiple distribution channels to maximize your reach. Utilize digital options including social media. Printed direct mailers are still useful as well as publishing articles through key public relations outlets. Lastly, it is very important to know which promotional efforts bring in your new prospects to maximize your future spending to maximize ROI.

There are many promotional techniques at your disposal such as offering:

- Free samples
- Free trials
- Product coupons and rebates
- Contest "give-a-ways"
- Limited pricing offers
- Key influencer testimonials
- Point of sale displays

How you position your product or service in the minds of your prospects and against the competition is also important. Avoid conflicting messages. Each promotion should focus on positive impact statements that address the following customer-related questions:

- What is in it for the user?
- How does the service make the user's work life easier and more successful?

- What unique benefits will the user obtain (e.g., growth, smarter decision-making, improved productivity, cost savings, greater market intelligence)?

- What unique features does the service bring vs. the competition?

Trying to promote the same product or service differently across unique and disparate market segments can be creative, can be cost effective, and can bring other benefits. But only until interactions and communications between customers in the different segments take place. Then, you will have some tough explaining to do as one promotion targeted to a particular user segment may not have been offered to another, upsetting them and potentially running them off.

On the other hand, trying to be "all things to all people" is not always credible. The product they chose for certain reasons may no longer meet their preconceived perceptions based on how you are now positioning it. Creating sub-brands may be a more concrete alternative to distinguish between promotions and allow for unique promotional positioning and less customer confusion or unhappiness.

4. Place

This component of your marketing mix concerns market reach and distribution via alternate sales channels. It addresses what sales channels you utilize to efficiently and cost effectively connect with your prospect/customer base. These usually fall under the scope and responsibility of the sales team. Consider all possible sales channels (e.g., field, phone, outside third-party sales agents, E-commerce, social media). A multi-faceted approach utilizing many of these distribution channels may be warranted.

While the cost to utilize each channel is important, it is also important to agree upon which channel is best to promote and sell each type of product or service. For example, selling a sophisticated higher priced consulting or data service usually requires multiple face-to-face prospect interactions. Video conferencing and virtual product demos work well, too. On the other hand, lower priced, higher volume products such as publications, training courses, and events may not require face-to-face interactions. The optimal sales channel for these are direct mailers, online ads, direct phone, or third-party sales agents. Successes can be achieved through these lower cost sales channels.

Lessons Learned

A former Sales Agent (SA) of ours had the sole rights to our Point of Sales (POS) data. This meant they controlled our complete customer relationship and contacts, not us. Without our knowledge, they decided to produce their own similar service to compete head-to-head with ours. They also misrepresented us by telling all customers our service (which was the market leader) would not be updated. They then offered theirs as a substitute to replace our so-called cancelled service.

We found all this out when we received a huge number of calls to our general office line from shocked customers. We immediately cancelled this SA agreement and initiated a mass marketing effort to alert all our users that we had no plans to discontinue this critical service. Unfortunately, we could not contact the customers directly because the SA had all the POS data.

We did take a short-term financial hit. It took us about two years of reaching out through global advertising to get our complete customer base back. On a side note, our former SA's product was discontinued. Poetic justice!

What is the lesson? Never give up your POS rights to any SA.

If you decide to promote the same product through multiple channels, you may encounter internal conflicts of interest if you operate separate sales teams per each channel. We operated separate field sales, direct phone sales, and online (social media) sales efforts, complimented by sales agents. What you want to avoid upfront is having these teams arguing over who gets the sales credit for a sale through their specific channel. One way to avoid this dilemma is to "ring-fence" which sales channels sell each product (avoiding duplication).

We created a product-channel grid to clarify this issue. Thus, whichever channel the sale goes through receives the credit. This grid also encouraged our sales team in one channel to pass along product leads to the sales teams, resulting in good teamwork and collaboration.

What are your thoughts?

Related to the BCG Growth Matrix, what percentage of your total product portfolio do you categorize within Stars, Question Marks, Cash Cows, and Dogs?

What specific tactics does your organization deploy to "lock-in" your key customers to prevent them from shifting to competition?

Can you easily explain your pricing strategies, policies, and practices (why or why not)?

Is each of your P&Ss clearly positioned against your key competitors with a well- articulated competitive advantage understood by prospects? How might such promotions be improved?

What multiple sales channels are used to reach your prospect/customer bases? Are additional options available to exploit (where and how)?

CHAPTER 16

Sales and Marketing

Chapter Preview

- How to maximize revenues through an effective Sales Management program, and which activities are paramount

- Key competencies and skill set of "top-rated" salespeople.

- Tips for qualifying sales prospects and improving results during sales calls.

- Marketing Management approaches and initiatives to attract and retain customers.

- The process to build a Brand and its Equity (value).

- The continued demand and exponential growth of eCommerce and other marketing trends to not overlook.

Sales is a product-oriented activity. These activities are usually one-on-one, people-driven relationships. The goal of sales is to maximize revenues by attracting and retaining new customers. This is achieved by successfully addressing their unique set of needs. Marketing focuses on customer-oriented activities and uses analytics to identify market opportunities. Marketing relies more on media sources to reach specific targeted segments or a mass market. Other goals of marketing include improving CSAT levels (see Chapter 6), increasing market share, and building brand awareness and loyalty.

Related to the "4 Ps" (see Chapter 15), the Sales function's primary responsibilities involve selling and securing "Products" through identifying the best means of distribution, otherwise known as sales channels or "Place." Marketing addresses the remaining two responsibilities of "Pricing and Promotion."

Sales Management

The Sales function is the main revenue-generation source within an organization. A key objective is to drive and grow the flow of P&Ss to customers.

Sales Management's primary focus is building and developing a sales team. Other activities include:

- Recruiting.

- Setting up a sales plan with market growth strategies.

- Devising individual sales territory coverage, either by geographic location, product, or market segment. A question to address is: "Based on your P&S portfolio, is there a market need for sales specialists (product experts), generalists (who sell all P&Ss alike), or a combination of both?"

- Establishing and supervising within a motivational work environment, including staff professional development, coaching, and career planning.

- Training on account sales strategies, building and qualifying a QP, establishing tactical sales techniques and tools, leveraging social media, gaining product knowledge, negotiating skills, securing referrals, developing account/relationship management skills, and maximizing account revenues.

- Target quota setting, tracking, and forecasting.

- Establishing compensation and incentive plans that drive the right behaviors and results (in consultation with HR and Finance).
- Pursuing alternate sales channels to improve market reach.
- Overseeing sales strategies, operations, administration, and analytics.

Sales Acumen

During my tenure in sales management, I created a simple "skills grid" or aptitude checklist to evaluate the progression of my individual team members. Sales experience and expertise should not be assessed solely based on longevity (e.g., number of years in sales). Such sales acumen should be judged by the level of competencies acquired as well as sales accomplishments achieved. There are "basic" and "advanced" selling skills that I categorize as follows:

Skills & Competencies	Knowledge Level	
	Basic	Advanced
Product Knowledge	generalist	specialist
Product Demo's	canned	customized
Market Intel	trends	competitive
Selling Skills	tactical	strategic
Sales Approach	product-focus	customer-focus
Sales Orientation	harvester	hunter
Relationship Mgt.	you know them	they know you
Target Achievement	usually meets	consistently exceeds
Training	needs development	train the trainer

Until I assessed that everyone on my team was at the advanced level, each was a "work in progress." Each salesperson progressed at their own pace, many becoming advanced in all categories within a very short timeline, while others were not so fortunate. If everyone had access to the same training programs and my coaching, why such a disparity?

I suggest the following rationale as to why certain individuals more quickly excelled to the advanced levels:

- Individuals have different preferences as to how they prefer to learn (see Chapter 8). Our training program catered to only a single learning methodology, which suited some better than others.

- Exhibited strong levels of both IQ and EQ (see Chapter 3).

- Culturally diverse and astute.

- Predominantly extroverted (vs. introverted).

- High level of self-confidence and competitive nature.

- Creative problem-solving ability.

- Inquisitive and active listener.

- Self-starter, self-motivated, high energy, and passion.

- Comfort and "fit" within the sales function and desire to assist others before themselves.

Is there one best approach to interact with prospects? In today's competitive global landscape, I say, "NO." Due to time and cost constraints, the need to grow your QP efficiently, while building relationships effectively, it is logical to combine certain selling methods with each prospect. These include face-to-face field contacts, direct sales by phone, and virtual sales demonstrations. How and when such hybrid selling models are implemented should be based on the specific selling cycle stage you are within (see Chapter 14).

For example, face-to-face and video conference meetings are an efficient and timely means of prospecting and building stronger relationships with higher dollar volume prospects. Conducting virtual product demos is another less costly sales method as compared to face to face. A follow-up phone call then provides a means to touch base and provides prospects with timely updates and additional information for proposals. Lastly, another face-to-face meeting may be required to negotiate and finalize contract terms based on the prospects' comfort level. Most post-sale activities can easily be concluded via phone, email, or text.

Lessons Learned

I know of very few competent salespeople who tend "NOT" to go where they know they have the best chance of making their sales quota and earning a nice bonus.

Even some of my most successful salespeople would shy away from selling a new product as it is a much more challenging and time-consuming sale. Thus, many of our new products were missing their respective revenue targets. We had to take action to gain a better balance of our field selling time.

Most sales activities and behaviors are driven by incentives and rewards as well as being within your comfort zone. Thus, we revised their total incentive/bonus plan to have 30% of it based on achieving NPD sales targets. While both are important, rewarding new business should take precedence over renewals. We also trained them to ensure they were more confident with our new product and its competition. They were not instantly thrilled, but they also recognized that if we never produced any new and successful products or services, they would eventually run out of things to sell. Behaviors slowly began to change as did new product revenues. Commitment and money talks.

This hybrid sales model is reinforced by a recent Bain and Co. Dynata study, [50] which found that 92 percent of potential business-to-business (B2B) buyers prefer virtual interactions, while field sales staff prefer the more traditional face-to-face meetings. While field sales teams that utilized virtual tools generally did not report any uptick in their closure rates or increase in revenues, they did observe lower sales costs whereby 79 percent of sellers surveyed gave virtual tools an "effective" rating. Also, field sales teams agreed that the virtual meeting method allows them to reach out to many more small-to-medium accounts that would not otherwise be able to justify more costly face-to-face interactions. This is advantageous when building your prospect list.

What makes a successful sales call? Here are a few of my tips (having participated in thousands of them). Never lead off a sales call by offering your most popular product or service. Instead, begin by asking your prospect to identify their biggest challenges hampering or preventing their success. In this way, you can identify their top business priorities and match these with your possible assistance and solutions.

Speak less, ask more questions, and listen! On the contrary, if you talk too much and get into the weeds, their eyes will begin to glaze over. You will know right then that you have gone on too long. Stop and quickly regroup.

Try your best to qualify the prospect upfront. But be sensitive to not offend them. Fair questions to ask include:

- What is the motivation behind the purchase?
- Who is (are) the decision maker(s)?
- What is the timeline and decision-making process?
- Is this potential purchase budgeted? If so, how much funding is available and the timeline for spending it?
- Have you identified any solutions that meet your needs?

> **Lessons Learned**
>
> Our consulting team sent out hundreds of prospect proposals annually with a meagre single-digit closure rate as most were not truly qualified. They could have spent their time billing hundreds of more hours in project delivery, making real money vs. drafting proposals.

Being asked to send a product proposal too early into a sales call is not always a good thing. Beware! You should be cautious about sending proposals before a more thorough prospect qualification. In many instances, the prospect may just be trying to placate and get rid of you. Or they know whom they prefer to do business with but need to collect at least three competitive bids (and you are one of them) to satisfy their own procurement department's bidding criteria.

One way to surmise if you are "being played" is to agree to send a detailed proposal on the condition that you schedule a follow-up call on an exact date and time to discuss the proposal's merits and receive their feedback. If they are noncommittal, pass. You will not only save the salesperson's time from wasted follow-up calls but save your product team's time creating needless detailed proposals.

One final tip, once you have earned the right, "ask for the business!" No deal is ever closed without doing so. Once all prospect issues, concerns, or objections have been successfully addressed, this is the next logical step. This step is known as a "trial close." The prospect either agrees to do business with you and then shift the discussion to post-sale issues, or they are hesitant, which means you still have work to do to uncover why. Never end a sales call without clarity as to exactly where things stand and without a timebound set of next steps.

Sales Operations

Sales operations cover the establishment of roles, consistent activities, and processes from a sales administration standpoint. Operations enable and support the sales team's activities by taking over responsibility for administrative and technical burdens from them. This allows the sales team to spend more time selling, shortening the sales cycle, and providing the product teams with valuable market and user insights. If the sales team identifies potential new sales partners (e.g., sales agents), operations steps in to finalize the relationship and monitor future progress.

A criterion for considering new sales agent channel distributors includes evaluating:

- Cost of sales (COS) by channel.
- Price points for high-value/low-volume products and low-value/high-volume products.
- Size and disparity of prospect bases at the global, regional, and local levels.
- Knowledge and understanding of the prospect (e.g.: who are they and what are their needs).
- Sharing POS details.
- Possessing a growth "pay for performance" mindset.

When working with a global sales team across multiple time zones, it is paramount that they possess the ability to negotiate and close new business "on the spot." This can be accomplished by creating specific Terms and Conditions (T&C) sheets for each product portfolio. The goal is to establish preapproved price discount ranges and acceptable contractual term revisions that the sales team can efficiently and effectively negotiate. This process saves time and builds greater sales team credibility with their customers. It should be noted that any prospect request outside such preapproved parameters will still require approval by Sales Management or higher management depending on the size of the contract.

Lessons Learned

In closing this sales discussion, I have heard a thousand times from my colleagues who are not in sales, "I do not sell." By this, they are implying they are uncomfortable with the concept and notion of how salespeople are sometimes negatively perceived. On the contrary, I always try to convince them that they actually do get involved in "selling" more often than they think. Unless you control all related factors of pending decisions, to get what you want, you must positively influence others. Whether it is selling yourself for a promotion, pitching a proposal, deciding where to dine out, or spending family money on something you want, you are always selling something. Like it or not, the more success you have in business is due to your abilities to sell, influence, and solve problems. Case closed.

There is no greater intrinsic feeling or self-gratification than when you assist someone in addressing or solving their serious challenges or problems. In business, I call this process "selling," as you are directly satisfying their needs. If you put your customer's interests, needs, and well-being first, mutual success will follow.

Marketing Management

This function involves the process of promoting the buying and selling of products and services through attracting and retaining customers. Over the years, marketing is shifting from a "Push" to a "Pull" approach as consumers want and have more control over what they hear and view. "Push" or outbound initiatives are proactively driven by your organization, while "Pull" or inbound activities are consumer activated.

Marketing teams may adopt "defensive" approaches to reduce customer turnover and increase loyalty, or they may pursue "offensive" approaches to attract new customers and increase purchase frequencies. A combination of both approaches should reap maximum benefits.

Lessons Learned

At times, I became displeased with our young Marketing team's efforts when I perceived they were not focusing their valuable time on the right activities. This became apparent when their peers started avoiding them, not involving them in key decisions, or going around them in areas that were their main responsibilities.

I took action. I set up a short exercise with them in the hopes of better guiding them where and how they should spend their time. I listed the main activities of marketing on a flip chart and asked them to collectively agree on how much time (a percentage), they dedicated to each. They allocated their percentages and were quite pleased that they had reached consensus. There were smiles all around the room. But it was mind-boggling for me, as my previous concerns were confirmed.

What they did not know was I had taken the same list of activities and wrote in what I believed was the appropriate time percentage that they should be dedicating to each activity. When I flipped over the chart of activities to my own percentages, it became mind-boggling for them as well. All smiles quickly disappeared. They were spending zero time on strategic market development and I expected 50 percent. They were spending 70 percent of their time on product marketing collateral design. I expected this to be 10 percent. They were conducting zero market research, competitive, or pricing analysis. I expected 25 percent. You get the picture.

We implemented the necessary priority changes as most of them were working within their respective comfort zones and focusing on the simplest tasks. Others were lacking some of the skill sets needed to perform the more complex tasks. We worked on both obstacles, and the marketing team later became more valuable colleagues. This peer feedback was gathered annually through a newly created internal customer satisfaction online survey. The peer satisfaction results were very high.

Marketing should not be viewed as an isolated function but as a way of doing business. To be successful, it needs to be embraced by the whole organization. To maximize its effectiveness, marketing initiatives should be embedded within other business activities (e.g., strategic planning, product development, NPD, and sales, etc.). Your marketing team can only reach and interact with a limited number of customers as resources are finite. However, if you can harness your non-marketing staff and their daily external touchpoints, you will be able to communicate your messaging with many more customers and prospects.

Various marketing approaches and activities include:

- **Relationship Marketing**—A one-on-one approach that provides individual and personal consumer attention. Its goal is to ensure each customer perceives they are very important and your main priority.

- **Smart Marketing**—An approach focused on attracting new business, client retention, and tracking satisfaction levels. It takes a long-term view focused on driving client equity, which is tracking the sum of the lifetime value that each client brings vs. just tracking short-term transactions.

- **Viral Marketing**—Expose consumers to your specific messaging in the hopes that they will "pass it on" to other consumers within their own networks.

- **Green Marketing**—Stresses that your overall organization as well as your products and services are environmentally safe and sensitive to ecological concerns.

- **Keyword Marketing**—Used for online search engines to reach the right audience with the right message at the right time. The goal is to be in the top placement in search results. Otherwise, you may get caught up in all the other online "noise and chatter" and receive very few hits or views.

In addition to overseeing Pricing and Promotion, other more traditional marketing activities include:

- Strategic Market Penetration and Development (see Chapter 13)
- Product Marketing
- Research and Competitive Analysis
- Social Media
- Advertising
- Corporate Marketing
- Public Relations
- Branding

Product Marketing

Product marketing occurs at the business level, focused on how to attract customers to each product. It encompasses the end-to-end process of bringing a product to market. This entails promotional positioning, messaging, launching and post-launch activities involved within each product's phase of its life cycle (e.g., introduction, growth, maturity, and decline). The goal is driving market demand and product usage.

Marketing Research

This activity gains insights as to market intelligence, opportunities, and your competitive positioning. It uncovers potential customer needs, problems, and monitors product performance. Conducting online market surveys are an economical and efficient means for gathering the "voice of the customer." If you do not possess the required internal expertise, the process can easily be outsourced with good results.

Social Media

This area has become a dominant force in business today due to its numerous economic benefits and brand reach. Social media's many advantages include accurate, efficient consumer research and engagement, building thought leadership, expanding lead generation, tracking ROI on your marketing spending and greater product innovation. It is a useful means to build upon your marketing contact database.

Consumers can now gain instant access to your product or service details, including sharing their feedback related to them. The sheer magnitude of this is huge. Pew Research [53] reinforces this point by indicating that approximately 85 percent of all Americans own a smartphone as of 2021. They now have instant access to your pricing, functionality details, quality reviews, and related competitive information. They can also easily share this information with others and engage with your customers and potential prospects within their social networks, blogs, chatrooms, etc.

These benefits will only materialize if your organization becomes an active part of the conversation and online communities. Active customer and prospect engagement on social media should assist you in accomplishing this.

With the right tools and applications in place, e-commerce offers great potential as an efficient and cost-effective, alternate sales channel.

Advertising

Also known as mass marketing, advertising is a nonpersonal marketing communication tool that brings the attention of the public to a company and its products and services. Much advertising is funded by sponsors who pay for space in print, broadcast media, billboards, online, or other means. The large expense associated with advertising can be difficult to justify if the ROI cannot be tracked directly to the results of each advertisement (by the secured new business from each ad campaign). Corporate advertising can be a useful outlet for building brand awareness and identity as well as in public relations campaigns.

Digital Marketing

These activities allow you to combine market research, social media, and advertising to achieve the goals of smart marketing which include new customer acquisition, retention, lifetime value, and loyalty. Digital marketing provides a means of better understanding customer preferences. It allows you to track and understand how and which prospects or customers interact with your direct email messages. You can also learn which of your website content is being viewed and what is their frequency. These become a source of new prospect leads for your various P&Ss, which can be passed along to your sales team for further engagement.

It has become very easy to calculate the actual ROI for each advertisement and makes it very clear how your average Customer Acquisition Cost (CAC) compares to your average Customer Lifetime Value (CLV). CAC costs include direct costs of advertising space, content creation and the costs of the marketing team members involved. Adding CLV into this mix allows you to maximize value vs. just focusing on costs. These are useful measures to assist in deciding where and how to invest future advertising dollars. In 2020, digital advertising spending reached $275 billion as compared to global TV ads at $160 billion. [54]

Corporate Marketing

The main purpose of corporate marketing is to communicate the organization's overall long-term strategies and goals. These include stakeholder or shareholder value creation, growth, diversification, expansion, stability, re-invention, etc. The keys to successful corporate marketing are about delivering the "right" message to the "right' audience, through the "right" medium at the "right" time to build or enhance the organization's brand equity or goodwill.

Public Relations (PR)

Similar to advertising, PR is a promotional method. But, while advertising focuses on pushing product sales, PR focuses on maintaining a quality public reputation. This is accomplished by informing and persuading the organization's various external constituents through utilizing press releases, conducting public forums, and presenting news clips, etc. Its ultimate success is based upon getting "positive" media coverage.

Branding

Branding is the "promise you make," while your Brand is the "promise you keep." A Brand can take many forms: a name, phrase, term, logo, symbol, packaging, etc. It distinguishes your product or organization from its competitors, which requires unique positioning. If successful, the Brand becomes an emotional and positively perceived image in the minds of consumers and something with which they strive to be associated. Negative impressions may also occur. As previously mentioned, advertising is one means of promoting your Brand. Success here is based on and measured by new customer adoption and retention.

The goal of branding is to move customers through the various steps or stages along the branding hierarchy (from Salience to Resonance). This process is described in detail by Kevin Keller, who created the Consumer-Based Brand Equity Model, which is illustrated by a branding pyramid with four levels or stages. [55] As an organization makes efforts to move customers up the branding pyramid (from bottom to top) of customer affiliation, your brand image should strengthen.

The four levels to be achieved in ascending order are:

Level 1: Salience—Is achieved at a basic level when consumers can identify and are aware of your Brand. Greater salience is achieved when consumers recall your Brand, in its absence, when in the presence of your competitors.

Level 2: Performance and Imagery—Occurs when consumers can differentiate the look and feel as well as the distinctive performance characteristics of your Brand.

Level 3: Judgements and Feelings—Occurs once the consumer can make rational or emotional judgements regarding your Brand. Such perceived judgments include quality, credibility, warmth, fun, excitement, and social approval. This also involves the consumer creating direct associations to your Brand. These may be related to other consumer groups, friends, family, and opinion leaders who also support the brand.

Level 4: Resonance—At this stage, the consumer becomes actively engaged with your Brand. Loyalty and advocacy come into play as consumers actively promote and recommend your Brand to others.

It should be noted that each of these four branding levels must be achieved in order before moving on to the next level. A level cannot be skipped. How much time it takes for consumers to ascend through all four levels is driven by the consumers themselves and based on the creative and proactive branding techniques of the organization.

Opinion leadership was brought to prominence by Paul Lazarsfeld, Elihu Katz and Robert Merton. [56] It explains the diffusion of innovation, ideas, and commercial products and services. Opinion leaders are usually not formally or directly associated with the commercial selling source of a Brand. However, they can be very influential of others. Their advice is usually given in casual, informal, and interpersonal conversations. This process is quite simple. There is an influencer (opinion leader) and an opinion receiver (potential buyer). This can also be iterative whereby the receiver becomes an opinion leader themselves.

Opinion leaders are viewed as credible, knowledgeable, and reliable sources of information, advice, and recommendations that are given with the best interest of the opinion receiver in mind. They possess distinct personality traits, such as self-confidence and gregariousness. They are generally extroverted, outspoken, and socially inclined. Their expert advice lessens a buyer's perceived risks and anxiety due to the opinion leader's perceived firsthand knowledge. Opinions shared can be of a favorable or unfavorable nature. Marketers refer to this process as "word of mouth" communication. Now, with the advent of technology (e.g., social media, email, chat rooms, texting), "word of mouth" is spreading like wildfire.

Advocates, as opposed to loyalists, actively take a strong position in support of, push for, and call for a particular cause. Loyalists focus more on the merits of a single product, service, or brand. The actions of both loyalists and advocates can even go so far as them assisting in the assembly of a Brand Community of content and happy users. An example of this phenomenon is the "HOG" club, the supporters of Harley-Davison Motorcycles. Such activities are the "Holy Grail" of branding.

Lessons Learned

It may sound illogical, but if you have no actual or perceived competition, you may want to consider creating some, as consumers prefer to compare product offerings. A good example of this is Intuit. A number of years ago, they successfully created a new, electronic personal tax filing service. The "competitor" they created was the traditional, long, and arduous "pencil and paper" method of filing your personal taxes. The rest is history.

When it comes to branding, competition is good and should be welcomed. Competition prevents complacency. Nor do you ever want to be perceived in the market as possessing a monopolistic position. Possessing such a dominant market position may be viewed as protectionism and possibly lead to anti-trust investigations. Such pricing and perceived anti-competitive practices may also come under legal scrutiny at such times. Avoid this at all costs.

> **Lessons Learned**
>
> "If you can't beat them, join them." Partnerships are a great alternative vs. going head-to-head with a strong competitor. Co-branding has become very popular, such as computer hardware run by "Intel inside." In today's competitive world, it is difficult to "do it alone."
>
> If you decide to partner, do not overuse a dominant position to "squeeze" them (with a win/lose contract). Even though a beneficial agreement is in place (for you), their inability to deliver on it could backfire on you. As a general rule, you should play fair with your competitors as you never know when you may want them as partners.

> **Lessons Learned**
>
> Desperate competitors can make foolish decisions that hurt the whole industry, particularly related to heavy price discounting that can drive down overall profit margins for everyone. But only if you choose to participate in such nonsense. Your goal should be to beat them, not eliminate them.

eCommerce continues to proliferate on a global scale. Many organizations are utilizing various marketing strategies to maximize this business opportunity by pursuing multiple target audiences. The sheer dollar volume of annual consumption and transactions via this platform speaks for itself with these four growing categories of:

- **B2B** (business-to-business)—Mainly involves the supply chain side of transactions (the purchase and sale of raw materials) as well as employee connections between organizations. These include producers, resellers, governmental, and various other institutions. Global B2B e-commerce Gross Merchandise Volumes (GMV) reached $26.7 trillion USD in 2020. [51]
- **B2C** (business-to-consumer)—Represents consumer consumption and is much smaller in total transaction amounts than B2B with a 2020 market size valued at $3.67 trillion USD. [52]
- **C2C** (consumer-to-consumer)—Involves consumers selling to each other, which is also growing rapidly (e.g., through Kijiji, eBay, etc.).
- **B2B2C** (business-to-business-to-consumer) - Involves selling to the end users of their business clients or to the employees of their client organization. Companies operating this model include Amazon and Walmart.

Future Trends

Many creative marketing trends are currently being rolled out while others are still in their infancy. Only time will tell which ones catch on and deliver their expected ROIs. Some of these newer trends include:

- **Conversational Marketing**—Using digital platforms to engage consumers in real time.
- **Voice Search Automation**—Addresses consumer questions via phone or online "chatbots" vs. "live" people.
- **Technological Fluency**—Involves language processing through neural networks, machine learning, or AI.

- **Analytics**—Using AI and algorithms with big data access.

- **Remote Talent Pools**—Leveraging or outsourcing marketing expertise through independent workers beyond the walls of your building.

- **Sensory Immersion**—We are in an environment of information overload, how do marketers better capture consumers attention? This can be achieved through interactive marketing experiences that focus on all five human senses.

More information and details on these and other marketing trends are just a click away. Have fun learning more online. [57]

Lessons Learned

Buying on emotion and then justifying the purchase to others in a more rational way does indeed occur. I offer personal proof. Many years ago, I was working our book exhibit at a publishing tradeshow. An individual came by our booth and pulled a book off our shelf and compared it to another book we published on the same topic, but under a separate Brand. He went into detail as to why he felt the book in his hand that he chose to use in his classroom was so much better than our other publication.

Here's the catch: both books had identical content (word for word) between their covers. The only difference was the branding of the two publishing labels. The one he selected had a stronger and more prestigious reputation.

I chose not to "rain on his parade" and did not have the heart to tell him the facts. I congratulated him on his "wise" decision, and he departed our booth a happy man.

What are your thoughts?

What changes can you suggest in improving the effectiveness of your sales organization (e.g., structure, geographic coverage, training, target setting, etc.)? Explain such related benefits.

List your top five skills or knowledge base a successful salesperson should possess. Why are these important than others?

What specific strategies and tactics do successful marketing teams execute well?

How effective is your organization's social media and digital marketing presence, and how can it be improved?

What percent of your total revenues are generated through eCommerce? How can it become a bigger part of your future revenue growth?

Does your marketing team track ROI on each advertising promotional campaign?

Related to the four levels of Brand Equity, have you achieved customer resonance? If not, what is your organizations current brand level and what steps do you suggest to ascent further up the branding pyramid?

What recommendations can you propose to your marketing team to pursue additional leading-edge technology trends and tools?

Part 3

Post-Script

Planning Your Future

As Ben Franklin said, "Fail to plan, plan to fail." The same can be said for managing your own career. Career development is a 50/50 proposition. You are responsible and own one-half and your organization owns the other half. But only you can decide who you want to be and where you want to go, not others.

You can achieve success on the job by delivering strong and consistent results as well as being more visible by befriending others. Living up to your commitments is critical. The same can be said for your personal life as well.

You can proactively put additional actions in place that will assist you on both fronts. Here are a few recommendations:

- Identify and perfect the leadership and management styles that you are comfortable with and align with your overall personality traits. Continue to practice these and be flexible and adaptive when situations change, requiring you to adjust. This becomes the foundation of who you are and how you work.

- Think about where you want to be (position-wise) in one to five years out. What does success look like at each incremental phase, both personally and professionally? If you are not happy at home, you probably will not be as productive at work.

- Discuss your aspirations with your supervisor or unbiased colleagues for a reality check. Reassess your plan annually. Remember, patience is a virtue. Hopefully, if your boss is honest and transparent, you will gain valuable feedback as to where you can improve and grow (in both hard and soft skills) for your future advancement. You will need to be open-minded and have thick skin to handle constructive criticism. However, if there are zero internal opportunities for you in the foreseeable future and you are truly ready to do more now, you may want to investigate opportunities outside your organization.

- Seek out a career coach or mentor whose advice you trust. They can play the key role of "carrying your flag," as self-promotion is usually not taken kindly. Practice, test, and apply the guidance you glean from them and learn from your mistakes. You should be able to seek their advice related to an external search. They can assist you in evaluating the pros and cons by asking you a series of questions only you can answer.

- Find ways to become more visible to your senior management team or board of directors. When opportunities exist, be prepared to ask them thoughtful questions and listen to their answers. Being inquisitive is seen as a good trait to possess.

- Volunteer for special projects that mean something to your organization, not just "busy" work. Being a team player and "utility" person who can always be called upon is a nice position to be in.

- Perfect the art of interviewing. Apply for select vacant positions even if you know you are not yet totally qualified. You will not only improve your interviewing skills but identify the areas and skills gaps that need your attention for the next time around as well.

- Expand and update your "Teachable Point of View" as your personal and professional life journey evolves. As MLB Hall of Famer Yogi Berra said, "It ain't over till it's over."

- Capitalize on organizational restructuring (re-orgs). View these as opportunities to take on new roles rather than viewing such changes as a threat. It has been said in relation to change that there are three types of people: those who ride the wave, those who duck under the wave, and those who are hit by it. Which one are you?

READ, READ, READ! The topic of Emotional Intelligence (EI) is a must as it can assist in putting your personal and professional lives in a better order. Search for additional material in areas where your interest is strong but your knowledge is weak or nonexistent. Suggestions include research on current and future market trends, relevant stats and data, key business strategies, concepts, frameworks, guidelines, tools, checklists, etc. The goal here is to become a "quick study" and not "reinvent the wheel" all by yourself. Benefit from other's work.

In summation, by building and applying learned leadership and management skills, it took me twelve years to achieve my career aspirations in my early thirties. My learning continues to this day. I hope I have been of assistance in sharing my career insights and wish you all the best as you consider your own path to self-actualization.

Lessons Learned

If/when you become successful, you may face an interesting dilemma of which path to take when faced with a career "fork in the road." Here is an example I faced early in my career:

I began my career in Sales and was quickly promoted to District Sales Manager, then Regional Sales Manager. I was then offered the VP of Sales position. I asked our CEO what he thought I should do. He said, "If you want a career in Sales then take it. But, if you aspire to one day sit in my chair, you need to learn about other sides of the business."

I turned down the VP offer and became a Product Manager, a two-level reduction based on our compensation and organization structure. I even had to turn in my company car! While taking a short-term financial hit, my spouse, Debi, understood the longer-term career prospects, believed in my future, and wholly supported our collective decision. My CEO's advice worked out as I eventually became the CEO (sitting in his chair)!

Author Bio

Mark Hubble has held numerous "C-suite" level and board-level positions. These include:

- President and CEO, Southwestern College Publishing
- President, Higher Education Group, Addison Wesley Longman
- CEO, Sheshunoff Information Services
- President, Compass Learning
- President, Education Online
- Senior Vice President, Commercial Aviation Solutions, International Air Transport Association (IATA)
- Senior Strategic Advisor, Premise Travel and Hospitality Group
- Board positions: Cargo Network Services, Beijing Information Technology Company (Chairman), IATA Netherlands BvD (Chairman)
- Strategic Advisor, Premise Data Corp. for Travel & Hospitality Group
- Lecturer: The University of Texas Austin, Texas State University, Concordia University (taught various graduate and undergraduate business courses in Leadership, Management, Marketing, Branding, and Strategic Human Resources Management)
- Taught corporate training seminars, workshops in Sales, Negotiations, Product Management, Stakeholder Management, Time Management, and Innovation within all his organizations.

- His business track record includes numerous corporate turnarounds and building high-performance teams that consistently delivered industry-leading profitable growth. Earlier in his career, he earned numerous top Sales and Product Management/Development honors.

- Education: BBA (Texas State U.) and MBA (St. Edwards U.)

- Executive Education: INSEAD France, Columbia University, NYC.

Bibliography

[1] Bok, Derek, C., *Quotations of Bok* (retrieved August 21, 2021), en.wikipedia.org/wiki/derek_bok

[2] Kaplan, R.S. (September 15, 2015), *What You Really Need to Lead: The Power of Thinking Exactly Like an Owner*, Boston, HBR

[3] Sinek, Simon, *Start with Why*, Penguin Random House, London, England (2009)

"Interview" (October 22, 2011), (retrieved June 10, 2021), www.lifeandleadership.com

[4] Willink, J., Babin, L. (20 October, 2015), *Extreme Ownership: How U.S. Navy SEALs Lead and Win*, NYC, St. Martin's Press

[5] Maxwell, J., *5 Levels of Leadership* (October 2011), NYC, Grand Central Publishing (September 2013), NYC, Center Street Publishing

[6] Welch, J. (April 26, 2018), *The Ingredients to Great Leadership*, Jackwelch.stryer.edu/winning/leadership

Welch, J., Welch, S., (2005), *Winning*, 1E., NYC, Harper Collins

[7] Doran, G., Miller, A. & Cunningham, J. (November 1981), MIT Cambridge, Management Review article

[8] Thompson, J. (September 30, 2011), *Beyond Words: Is Nonverbal Communication a Numbers Game?* www.psychologytoday.com

[9] Tichy, N. (2002, 2004), *The Cycle of Leadership: How Great Leaders Teach Their Companies to Win*, NYC, Harper Collins

[10] Weiler, R. & Brimstone Consulting (July 1, 2020), *The Core 4: Harnessing 4 Core Business Drivers to Accelerate Your Organization*, Kindle Edition

[11] Brooks, D., (April 21, 2015), *The Road to Character*, NYC, Random House

[12] Wooden, J. (September 28, 2015), *Woodenisms*, (retrieved May 15, 2021) www.thewoodeneffect.com

[13] Golemen, D., Boyatzis, R. & Mckee, A. (2013), *Primal Leadership: Realizing the Power of Emotional Intelligence*, Boston, Harvard Business Press.

Emotional Intelligence: Why It Can Matter More Than IQ, (September 1, 1995), NYC, Bantam Books (Penguin).

[14] Plum, E., (2008), *Cultural Intelligence (CI)*, London, Libri Publishing and (2008),

Cultural Intelligence: The Art of Leading Cultural Complexity, UK, MU Press

[15] Hofstede, G., (1965, 1973, 1990–2002, 2010), *Cultural Dimensions Theory*, Europe, IBM and *Cultural Consequences* (1984), Beverly Hills, SAGE Publishing

[16] Cruz, M. (2014), Article, *Gen Y Workplace Needs and Preferred Leadership Styles*,

Ahmad, H., Ibrahim, B. (2014–15), *Leadership and the Characteristics of Different Generational Cohort towards Job Satisfaction*, Malaysia, Elsever Science Direct

Duquesnoy, P. (June 2021), *Generations, Leadership Styles and Employee Performance*, Netherlands, Tilburg Univ.

Kraus, M., (2017), *Comparing Gen X & Gen Y on Their Preferred Emotional Leadership Style*, the *Journal of Applied Leadership and Management*.

[17] Prahalad, C.K., Hamil, G., (May 1989), *Strategic Intent*, Boston, HBR

[18] Stewart, R., Humphry, A. (1966, 1973), *SWOT* article, Palo Alto, Stanford Research Inst.

[19] Kaufman, R. (August 7, 2012; October 13, 2018), *Uplifting Service: The Proven Path to Delighting Your Customers*, NYC, Evolve Publishing, RonKaufman.com

[20] Kotler, P. (1999), *Kotler on Marketing*, NYC, Simon Schuster, Principles of Marketing 6E, (2014), NYC, Simon Schuster, *Marketing Management: Analysis, Planning, Implementation & Control* 9E, (1997) NYC, Prentice Hall

[21] Griffin, A., Hauser, R. (1998), *VOC* article, Ill., Univ. of Chicago, Cambridge, MIT

[22] Amaresan, S. (February 19, 2021), *40 CSAT Stats to Know in 2021* (retrieved June 2021), https://blog.hubspot.com

[23] Lusty, K. (July 19, 2021), *Customer Engagement and Loyalty Stats* (retrieved September 1, 2021), accessdevelopment.com

[24] Goran (March 10, 2021), *40 Amazing Customer Loyalty Stats in 2021* (retrieved September 2, 2021), smallbizgenious.net

[25] Claussen, P. (April 2020), *Learn the Three Rs of Customer Loyalty* (retrieved September 1, 2021), Germantown, business.hughes.com

[26] Reichheld, F., Bain & Co., (1993, 2003), *NPS System*, Boston

[27] Gallo, C. (2021), *The Innovation Secrets of Steve Jobs*,

[28] Dyer, J., Gregersen, H., & Christensen, C. (July 19, 2011), *The Innovators DNA: Mastering the 5 skills of Skills of Disruptive Innovators*, Boston, Harvard Business Press, Article (October 2009), Boston, Harvard Business Review

[29] Patel, S. (July 16, 2015), *8 Successful Products That Only Exist Because of Failure* (retrieved September 3, 2021), www.forbes.com

[30] Christensen, C. (June 11, 1997), *The Innovators Dilemma: When New Technologies Cause Greats Firms to Fail*, Boston, HBR Press

[31] Rimol, M. (July 14, 2021), *Gartner Research Press Release*,

[32] Harari, O. (1996), Lesson 6, govleaders.org/powell/.htn, *The Powell Principle: 24 Lessons from Colin Powell a Legendary Leader*, 1E. (December 6, 2003), NYC, McGraw Hill, *The Leadership Secrets of Colin Powell* 1E. (February 18, 2012), NYC, McGraw Hill

Koltz, T. (May 22, 2021), *It Worked for Me: In Life and Leadership*, NYC, Harper

[33] Philips, D. T. (1992), *Lincoln on Leadership*, Ill., Hachette Book Group

[34] Beckingham, M. (March 2005), *What Great Managers Do*, Boston, HBR

[35] Bandura, A. (1970s), *3 Key Concepts of Social Learning Theory, 5 Essential Steps*, (January 6, 2020), Palo Alto, Stanford Univ.

[36] Manktelow, J., Birkinshaw, J. (October 24, 2018), *Top 10 Management Skills You Need*, Moss, D., shrm.org/hr, *Mind Tools for Managers: 100 Ways to be a Better Boss*, (2008), NJ, John Wiley & Sons

[37] Drucker, P. (October 16, 1954), *The Practice of Management*, (revised October 3, 2006), NYC, Harper Business

Bibliography

[38] Toegel, I. (November 2017), https://www.imd.org, Harter, J. (February 28, 2020), Workplace, https;//www.gallup.com, Mcevory, K. (August 4, 2016), keith.mcevory.com (retrieved August 27, 2021)

[39] Prosser, D. (July 3, 2005), *Thirteeners*, Austin, Greenleaf Publishing Group,

Norton, D., Kaplan, R., (September 1, 1996), *The Balanced Scorecard*, Boston, HBR,

[40] Jobs, S. (January 2, 2021, reproduced), marketmegood.com/blog/steve-jobs-leadership-quotes, (retrieved June 20, 2021)

[41] Dyer, J., Godfrey, P., Jensen, R. & Bryce, D., *Strategic Management: Concepts and Cases* 3E (n.d.), NY, John Wiley

[42] Porter, M. (1980), *Competitive Strategy* (1985), *Competitive Advantage*, NYC, Free Press, Simon Schuster

[43] Mitnick, R. S. (1973), *Agency Theory*, Jensen, M., Meckling, W. (Oct.1976), *Agency Theory*

[44] Neumann, J. v., Morgenstern (1940s), Shapley, L. S. (1962), *Game Theory*

[45] Boehm, B., Martin, J. (1991), *Rapid Application Development*, IBM, Bain & Co. (1996), *RAPID Decision-Making Model*, Boston

[46] Ansoff, I. (September to October 1957), *Strategies for Diversification*, p114, Boston, HBR

[47] Cooper, R., Kaplan, R., (May to June 1991), *Profit Priorities for Activity-Based Costing*, Boston, HBR, Vliet, V., Cooper, R. (2010), *ABC* (retrieved August 31, 2021), https;//www.toolshero.com/toolshero/robin-cooper

[48] McCarthy, J.E. (1960), *Basic Marketing: A Management Approach*, Ill., J.D. Irwin Publishing

[49[Henderson, B. (1968), *Growth-Share Matrix*, Boston Consulting Group, Boston

[50] Khandelwal, S., Deming, D., Hjortegaard, J. & Cruse, W. (April 2, 2021), *Virtual selling has become simply selling*, Bain & Co. and Dynata, bain&co.com (retrieved September 2, 2021)

[51] UNCTAD.org (May 3, 2021), *Global B2B GMV for 2020* (retrieved September 3, 2021)

[52] Grandviewresearch.com (March 2021), *2020 B2B Market Size* (retrieved September 3, 2021)

[53] Pewresearsch.org. (April 27, 2021), *Mobile Fact Sheet* (retrieved September 4, 2021)

[54] Visualcapitalist.com/evolution-global-advertising-spend-1980–2020 (retrieved February 28, 2022)

[55] Keller, K., Swaminathan, V. (August 15, 2019) *Strategic Brand Management* 5E, NYC, Pearson

[56] Lazarsfeld, Katz, E. (1957), *Personal Influence*, NYC, Free Press, Merten, R. (1957), *Social Theory and Social Structure*, NYC, Glencoe (Free Press), en.wikipedia.org/wiki/opinion_leadership# references (retrieved September 4, 2021)

[57] Dave, N. (n.d.), *42 Digital Marketing Trends You Can't Ignore in 2021*, https://singlegrain.com, (retrieved September 4, 2021)

CPSIA information can be obtained
at www.ICGtesting.com
Printed in the USA
LVHW010135240922
729163LV00012B/1073